THE CHURCH OF MODESTO

Dear, you + Him,
God bless you
as you serve Him,
Psalm 133:1-3
Jim Burck

THE CHURCH OF MODESTO

A City's Journey
Towards Christ Centered Unity

by Jim Bouck

Glenhaven Press   Modesto — 1999

THE CHURCH OF MODESTO
A City's Journey Toward
Christ-Centered Unity

by Jim Bouck

Published by:

GLENHAVEN PRESS
2401 E. Orangeburg Ave.
Suite 675 - 109
Modesto, CA 95355

Scripture taken from the HOLY BIBLE, NEW INTERNATIONAL VERSION®.
Copyright © 1973, 1978, 1984 by International Bible Society. Used by permission
of Zondervan Publishing House. All rights reserved.

First Edition

First Printing — May, 1999

1   2   3   4   5

Publisher's Cataloging in Publication Data
Bouck, James R.
The Church of Modesto, One Lord – One Church

Bibliography: p.

1. Religion – Christianity–Churches 2. U.S., California, Greater
Modesto Ministerial Assn. 3. Ecumenicity–United in prayer
4. Racial reconciliation, disaster relief, evangelism, community
action, 5. Interviews–history of the movement.

Library of Congress Catalog Card Number: 98-75647

Paperback   ISBN   0-9637265-9-5

Typeset with PTI LaTeX
Font: ITC Souvenir Light
Cover Art by Todd Graphics

ACKNOWLEDGMENTS

Special thanks to Shirley Williams for many hours of transcribing interviews. To Sid Freshour for his commitment to steer his publishing company in the direction of Christian ministry and for making this book happen. I especially want to thank my wife, Ann who has encouraged and assisted each step of the way.

Photos are from the author's collection unless noted otherwise.

The Body, Chuck Colson, Copyright ©1997, Word Publishing, Dallas, Texas. All rights reserved. Used by Permission.

Just As I Am, Billy Graham, Harper Collins, 1997. All rights reserved. Used by permission.

C.S. Lewis quotes from *The Quotable Lewis* Copyright ©1989, Wayne Martindale and Jerry Root, editors. Used by permission of Tyndale Publishers, Inc. All rights reserved.

In the Grip of Grace, Max Lucado, Copyright ©1996, Word Publishing, Nashville, Tennessee. All rights reserved. Used by Permission.

The Awesome Power of Shared Beliefs, Glenn Wagner, Copyright ©1997, Word Publishing, Dallas, Texas. All rights reserved. Used by Permission.

The Church of Modesto

TABLE OF CONTENTS

The Church of Modesto

TABLE OF CONTENTS

Chapter 1

INTRODUCTION
TO THE CHURCH OF MODESTO

A. A BACKGROUND ON
THE AUTHOR'S INTEREST IN THE TOPIC

I FIRST MOVED to Modesto in 1983. After ten years of living in the Los Angeles area and a two-year ministry in the city of Anchorage, I was ready for a smaller town lifestyle. My Alaska experience as a single-adults pastor led me to First Baptist Church where I served in their singles ministry with Pastor Jim Talley. When I first arrived there, it was a very exciting place to be. It had received much recognition from a decade of remarkable growth as well as their Institute in Church Imperatives (ICI), which attracted people from all over the world wishing to glean ideas from their success.

It seemed I had stumbled onto the best place to live this side of heaven. There was good preaching, scores of home Bible studies, a successful evangelism program, and hundreds of Christians meeting nearly every day of the week somewhere in its realm. It was so good there I could not imagine why anyone in Modesto would want to attend any other church. Personally I felt a sense of pride and rightness about my new church. After all, not only did we have it all figured out, we had it all down on paper and were teaching others how to "do" church. God must certainly be proud of our church! Occasionally however, it would disturb me when I would hear of people moving to other churches in

The Author's Family — Jim Jr., Ann, Jim and Josh.

town. I could not understand why, but usually it was fueled by some sort of discontent.

The news which troubled me the most was a move to another rapidly growing church, Big Valley Grace (How ironic that today I serve as a pastor there). Certainly God was at work in that church, but let them grow without our help. I also felt a little uneasy when some personal friends from a smaller church in town had the same criticism of the larger churches. They felt the big churches were stealing sheep from their church. Looking back, I am sure those feelings were shared by many people in Modesto during the 70s and 80s. God was on the throne, or thrones, of all the churches in Modesto.

However, each one represented a separate kingdom. The truth is, God was at work tilling the soil for the growth of unity during that entire time, long before I ever moved here. Just as God prepared the world for the Messiah's arrival in Bethlehem, He was preparing Modesto for a movement of unity. As the prophet, Haggai, wrote in Haggai 1:5:

> *"Is it a time for you yourselves to be living in your paneled houses, while this house remains a ruin?"* Now this is what the LORD Almighty says: *"Give careful thought to your ways. You have planted much, but have harvested little. You eat, but never have enough. You drink, but never have your fill. You put on clothes, but are not warm. You earn wages, only to put them in a purse with holes in it."* This is what the LORD Almighty says: *"Give careful thought to your ways. Go up into the mountains and bring down timber and build the house, so that I may take pleasure in it and be honored,"* says the LORD. *"You expected much, but see, it turned out to be little. What you brought home, I blew away. Why?"* declares the LORD Almighty. *"Because of my house, which remains a ruin, while each of you is busy with his own house. Therefore, because of you the heavens have withheld their dew and the earth its crops. I called for a drought on the fields and the mountains, on the grain, the new wine, the oil and whatever the ground produces, on men and cattle, and on the labor of your hands."*

"While each of you is busy with your own house." Ouch, that hurts, but what an accurate description that was of the churches in Modesto. Yet what a remarkable difference between that Modesto and the Modesto of 1998!

The churches in Modesto were extremely busy building their own houses, enlarging their own attendances, filling their own programs, and unfortunately with few exceptions, most of the time as Haggai pointed out, their harvests were small. Why? Because God's house remained a ruin. God was withholding the dew until we got it right, until we saw His temple, His house as more important than our own individual sanctuaries. His house was composed of more than our own separate congregations. For us, His house meant the Church of Modesto. We now realize He wanted one church in Modesto, one church with many congregations. Once we began getting unity down, the rains began to fall. Showers of blessings, beyond comprehension.

This book is a record of those blessings. It is a series of interviews which document the handiwork of the Lord in Modesto over the past fifty years.

Though the following illustration is lengthly, I believe it bears repeating as a description of the churches in Modesto before the current movement of unity. In his book *In The Grip Of Grace*, Max Lucado tells the story of "Life Aboard the Fellowship":

> God has enlisted us in His navy and placed us on His ship. The boat has one purpose–to carry us safely to the other shore.
>
> This is no cruise ship; it's a battleship. We aren't called to a life of leisure; we are called to a life of service. Each of us has a different task. Some, concerned with those who are drowning, are snatching people from the water. Others are occupied with the enemy, so they man the cannons of prayer and worship. Still others devote themselves to the crew, feeding and training the crew members.
>
> Though different, we are the same. Each can tell of a personal encounter with the Captain, for each has received a personal call. He found us among the shanties of the sea port and invited us to follow him. Our faith was born at the sight of His fondness, and so we went.
>
> We each followed Him across the gangplank of His grace onto the same boat. There is one captain and one destination. Though the battle is fierce, the boat is safe, for our captain is God. The ship will not sink. For that, there is no concern.
>
> There is concern however, regarding the disharmony of the crew. When we first boarded we assumed the crew was made up of others like us. But as we've wandered these decks, we've encountered curious converts with curious appearances. Some wear uniforms we've never seen, sporting

styles we've never witnessed. "Why do you look the way you do?" we ask them.

"Funny," they reply. "We were about to ask the same of you."

The variety of dress is not nearly as disturbing as the plethora of opinions. There is a group, for example, who clusters every morning for serious study. They promote rigid discipline and somber expressions. "Serving the captain is serious business," they explain. It's no coincidence that they tend to congregate around the stern.

There is another regiment deeply devoted to prayer. Not only do they believe in prayer, they believe in prayer by kneeling. For that reason you always know where to locate them; they are at the bow of the ship.

And then there are a few who staunchly believe real wine should be used in the Lord's Supper. You'll find them on the port side.

Still another group has positioned themselves near the engine. They spend hours examining the nuts and bolts of the boat. They've been known to go below deck and not come up for days. They are occasionally criticized by those who linger on the top deck, feeling the wind in their hair and the sun on their face. "It's not what you learn," those topside argue. "It's what you feel that matters."

And, oh, how we tend to cluster.

Some think once you're on the boat, you can't get off. Others say you'd be foolish to go overboard, but the choice is yours.

Some believe you volunteer for service; others believe you were destined for the service before the was ship was even built.

Some predict a storm of great tribulation will strike before we dock; others say it won't hit until we are safely ashore.

There are those who speak to the captain in a personal language. There are those who think such languages are extinct.

There are those who think the officers should wear robes, there are those who think there should be no officers at all, and there are those who think we are all officers and should all wear robes.

And, oh, how we tend to cluster.

And there is the issue of the weekly meeting at which the Captain is thanked and His words are read. All agree on it's importance, but few agree on its nature. Some want it loud, others quiet. Some want ritual, others spontaneity. Some want to celebrate so they can meditate; others meditate so they can celebrate. Some want a meeting for those who've gone overboard. Others reach those overboard but without going overboard and neglecting those on board.

And, oh, how we tend to cluster.

The consequence is a rocky boat. There is trouble on deck. Fights have broken out. Sailors have refused to speak to each other. There have even been times when one group refused to acknowledge the presence of others on the ship. Most tragically, some adrift at sea have chosen not to board the boat because of the quarreling of the sailors.

"What do we do?" we'd like to ask the captain. "How can there be harmony on the ship?" We don't have to go far to find the answer.

On the last night of his life Jesus prayed a prayer that stands as a citadel for all Christians:

I pray for these followers, but I am also praying for all those who will believe in Me because of their teaching. Father, I pray that they can be one. As you are in Me and I am in you, I pray that they can also be one in us. Then the world will believe that you sent Me. (John 17;20)

How precious are these words. Jesus, knowing the end is near, prays one final time for His followers. Striking, isn't it, that He prayed not for their success, their safety, or their happiness. He prayed for their unity. He prayed that they would love each other.

As He prayed for them, He also prayed for "those who will believe because of their teaching." That means us! In His last prayer Jesus prayed that you and I be one." [1]

Jesus prayed for their unity and He continues to pray for our unity even today! Few things bring Him greater joy than, as Psalm 133 describes, seeing brothers dwell together in unity.

Chris Baltzley, a missionary serving with The Navigators Organization in central Asia, recently relayed the following incident. "A group of missionaries sat in a planning meeting in the central Asian city of Bishkeck, the capitol of Kyrgystan. 'Did you say your supporting church was from Modesto? What's happening there? Isn't there some kind of revival going on in the churches there?'" The word is out and what God is doing in Modesto is being noticed in some pretty far reaching places. God is moving in this city with a Spirit of unity which is spreading throughout the world.

This book is a response to that question. "Isn't there some sort of revival going on in Modesto?" The answer is a resounding, "Yes!" God is moving in the hearts of the churches and pastors to create one community-wide church, the Church of Modesto. No, churches are not completely abandoning their individual identity; however, they are learning what it is to live as members of a greater community of believers. Perhaps Modestans are tasting what the early church experienced in their own citywide churches. Yes, God is moving in Modesto to create a community-wide church where pastors pray together weekly, Christians from different congregations fellowship and pray together regularly, and God's Spirit still does incredible things frequently.

Each chapter in this project records one facet of this remarkable story. The story of an awesome God, using ordinary people with average pastors, living in an inconspicuous town situated in a spiritually degenerate state. He has chosen to move this way in Modesto of all places, because as Nathaniel queried Philip: *"Can any good thing come out of Nazareth?"* People will ask the same of Modesto. When God moves in places like Modesto, there will be no doubt it was God at work and not man.

It is interesting to note that in 1995, a national survey[2] placed Modesto number 299 out of 300 on "America's most

desirable towns to live in". "Has not God made foolish
the wisdom of the world?" (1 Corinthians 1:20). Yes, God
does have a sense of humor. The point being, if there is a
revival in Modesto, God has positioned Himself to receive
all the Glory, which He rightly deserves. In collecting these
interviews it has been my privilege to hear first-hand, story
after story of God stirring hearts and orchestrating events.
I have become convinced, as I am sure you will, that He
has a special calling on the Church of Modesto. A calling
for us to be a leader in unity, maybe even an example for
other communities to learn from, or ministerial associations
to follow. The bottom line is this, God has chosen to do
something special in Modesto. He is the source, the insti-
gator, the leader, and the purpose of all that has occurred
here. I am confident that each pastor in Modesto would
echo these words. Apart from God's Spirit working in this
community, the following reports would not have occurred.
God is the source and the ongoing focus of Modesto's unity.

B. METHODOLOGY

The "Church of Modesto" is, in essence, many, many relationships; between pastors and pastors, pastors and paris-
honers, missionaries and church members, and between
parachurch organizations and churches, to name a few.

This study is the author's final product for the Doctor of
Ministry Degree from Western Seminary, Portland Oregon.
The objective is to present as many facets of the Church of
Modesto as possible, and then attempt to identify any con-
cepts which might transfer to another community's churches.
In order to do this, the methodology which best provides an
objective and detailed look at the relationships within COM
is by using an interview format. Therefore each chapter

is a presentation of one or more interviews with community leaders who relate their personal experience with the Church of Modesto. Each interviewee is asked a series of the same nine questions (See appendix), during a taped interview which was then transcribed.

C. INTERVIEW WITH MODESTO
CITY MAYOR, DICK LANG [3]

The following interview with Mayor Dick Lang is to gain some insight into the city leaders' perspective on the Church of Modesto. Do they recognize any special momentum within the Greater Modesto Ministerial Association? Is our recognition of this movement only within the Christian subculture, or is God truly touching our city through His church? Mayor Lang's interview sheds some light on this question. Therefore, in order to validate the reality of the Church of Modesto in the minds of the city leaders, I have included the following interview.

Q. Mayor Lang, please give a brief background on your life. I think people would be interested in knowing something about your personal life.

A. I was born here in Modesto some years ago, in 1937. The old St. Mary's Hospital, which is now City Hospital Rehab. [Rehabilitation]. But when I was a small boy we moved to Fresno with my dad's business. I went all through school in Fresno, including Fresno State. It was a wonderful experience. I have two older brothers, and we were all very active in sports and student leadership. In fact, I have a brother who's 360 days older than I am. My mother used to say twins the hard way. We were both student body presidents at our large high school in Fresno, Roosevelt High, and

— City of Modesto

Modesto City Mayor, Dick Lang.

both members of the debate team. We were both student body officers at Fresno State. In that sense I've always been kind of in the public eye.

I received my Bachelor's Degree in Political Science, and my Master's Degree is in Systems Management from Fresno State. I've always had a deep interest in the political process. Of course, through my life now I've been able to satisfy both my professional commitment to education as well as my quest for political activity.

My childhood was very stable. I lived in the same home for twenty two years. We had a good ride. It was a great family, and it was a very loving caring family. As you get older you appreciate the kind of environment you had previously.

I came to Modesto in 1960. My mother was born in Turlock. My grandparents on her side of the family had settled in Turlock in 1898. Their name is Crowell, and there's a school named after my grandfather. He was mayor of Turlock, and he was a community leader for years and years. My wife and I liked this area. In 1968 I decided to go into teaching and started with the Modesto City School system. It's the only system I've ever been with.

Q. Did they have church involvement at all?

A. Oh yes. My great grandfather was a Methodist minister, on my mother's side of the family. We were brought up in the church. I personally received Christ as a young teen. In fact, after we were married — we were married at the First Methodist Church in Fresno — my wife and I were the chaperons for what we called the MYF, Methodist Youth Fellowship, the junior high and high school kids. Through our lives, I am very pleased to say that our children have continued that involvement in the church in a variety of different ways. We feel very strongly about a Christian home and being Christians. I'll share with you some ways in which it has spilled over into my secular role as Mayor of this city. But education was always the very favorite thing of mine, and so we did go with the Modesto City School system. I was a Political Science major, so it was no surprise that I started teaching Government. For a while I also taught Competitive Speech because I had been varsity debater at Fresno State for four years. We now have three grown children and ten grandchildren. We feel very blessed about that. In 1976, then Mayor, Lee Davies got a hold of me. I was the Vice-Principal at Roosevelt Junior High School at the time. I had finished my teaching experience and had gone on into Administration. He called upon me to be chairman of the Bicentennial Celebration in Modesto. Unable to say no, I found myself chairing and directing ninety six different community events over a period of eighteen months, which was a wonderful and very patriotic experience. When I completed that, the Mayor said, "Lang, you'd better run for the Council." Unfortunately, again I was unable to say no, so I did [run]. I was first elected to the Modesto City Council in 1977, which is twenty one years ago. I was on the Council as a Council Member for thirteen years, appointed Mayor in '91, and then reelected twice since that time. So my total service is twenty two years. I'll probably run for one more term as Mayor. My collective community commitment will be in excess of a quarter of a century. It's been a wonderful, wonderful experience. My wife and I always feel very blessed that we've been able to serve the community in so many ways. In a nutshell, that's my personal background.

Q. Would you describe your relationship with the GMMA [Greater Modesto Ministerial Association] and are you happy with the work they are doing in Modesto?

A. Absolutely.   The GMMA is a very active group. It's grown.   When I first was associated with them, there were forty or fifty ministers.   The Church of Modesto, which evolved actually from the GMMA, is now in excess of ninety churches throughout our community.   Over the years, as a member of the City Council, we have called upon the GMMA to assist, promote efforts that we're doing to upgrade and enhance the moral fiber of our community, and many things that we can do. They've done that. We are so pleased that your Senior Pastor, David Seifert, has been a key person in that. Also Wade Estes of First Baptist [Church], Glenn Berteau of Calvary Temple, and a number of other ministers who are very key. It's a most impressive group, and frankly I don't know of another community in America that has the kind of relationship and common effort that we have here in the Modesto Area.

Q. Now, when you say that, it sounds like you've had some discussion and dialogue with other mayors.

A. Oh, we do that.   Frequently when we have Mayor-oriented conventions in Modesto, I will mention the Greater Modesto Ministerial Association to them. Pastors will be there and [the Mayors] will come up and ask them about . . .

Q. When you have other Mayors here?

A. That's right. They're jealous of what we can do. We've been able to do some things in Modesto that we're very proud of, and the churches, through GMMA, have done a great job in assisting us. We have, for instance,

what I consider to be probably the finest Adult Enter-
tainment Ordinance in the state of California. It's very,
very stringent. It has continually been challenged in
court, yet unsuccessfully. We get requests from all over
the State. We got a request from Thornton, California, wanting a copy of it because essentially we have
been able to eliminate the so called "Juice Bars," which
are a way of getting around ordinances. All but one
of the adult book stores, which is also kind of on the
demise, [are gone]. We see no social redeeming value
to have those kinds of enterprises or businesses. We
love free enterprise but only for those things that have
some goodness to them in terms of a contribution. I
will tell you that the churches, through GMMA and others, have been very, very supportive of our efforts in
that entire field and many other areas. It's so reassur-
ing to us as secular leaders to have religious leaders
in our community who are willing to step forward, express support for community and it's activities. I think
I'm the envy of a lot of mayors!

Q.   That's great to hear. Along with that, have you seen
any impact on the community as a result of the Church
of Modesto? You just mentioned the Ordinance, but
can you think of some impact that the Church of
Modesto has made on our community?

A.   There has been a multitude of things. Two or three
that come to mind immediately. About two years
ago, through closed circuit television, we had days
of prayer. One of those were set aside for Municipal
Leaders, and through that we had thousands of people in our community praying for our leadership. You
know, it does make a difference. It reassures us that
there are people there who want us to do the right
thing and are supporting us in that effort. I can't re-

member exactly what they called it now, but they went out nights and talked to five or so of their neighbors.

Q. Pray Greater Modesto?

A. Pray Greater Modesto. You're right. Thanks for reminding me. That has been just wonderful. And that's been an ongoing thing. The Church of Modesto, this consortium of ninety three or ninety four churches at this point, does a number of things. One of them in recent times focused on reconciliation. I declared February as the month of reconciliation. Now there's a number of our churches working very hard to keep families together, and for the reasons that we obviously all know, because where there is a strong family unit there is a stronger community. They have done a magnificent job on that. I attended probably six different churches during that month [of reconciliation]. As I told my wife, I've been double dosed all week attending two services, but I was at Big Valley Grace Community Church, and St. Paul's Episcopal Church, and all over the community as much as I could be.

Consequently the divorce rate in Modesto is much lower than the national average. Part of that we attributed to the fact of the efforts of reconciliation. That was a community-wide effort. In fact, I remember I kidded Pastor Seifert that I got writer's cramp. I signed 93 original proclamations so that every church in the Church of Modesto could have a Proclamation.

They also do things like the flood relief following the bad floods of January '97. That was a very devastating time in our community. The Tuolumne River flooded and we had over 300 homes flooded out with over 1,400 people displaced. But the churches came together as one unit. They had a warehouse down here where supplies were generously donated. People would come from all over to help and assist. What a magnificent expression of solidarity and genuine caring for their fellow man. I will tell you that in the midst of tragedy came so much inspiration because of the reaction of your people. And the Church of Modesto really did wonderful things for this community. I think it brought us to a new and higher level where we were tighter than ever in terms of the goodness of our community.

One day a year ago I was sitting in a local restaurant having breakfast with my wife, and two gentlemen came up to ask if I was Mayor Lang. I indicated I was. One was from Texas and the other from Alabama. They were out here looking at the Church of Modesto program because they had heard about it and wanted to start something in their respective states. You should know, as we know, that the efforts of the Church of Modesto are known nationwide.

Q. What is the attitude of the City Council as a whole towards the Ministerium and towards the Church of Modesto. Do they appreciate the fact that they've got some fairly Evangelical Guys praying at the beginning of these council meetings? Do they just tolerate it, or do they embrace it?

A. They embrace it. We think that having that spiritual guidance at the start of each meeting and a reminder of our commitment to God is a very, very important thing. It is good for us as community leaders to express to our citizens that we believe in it. You know, it's interesting. Some cities have taken prayer out of their city council meetings. Berkeley for instance has removed prayer. But Berkeley is Berkeley! We had a gentleman come in about three years ago. I don't recall his name, but he got to the roster one night. He said, "Mayor, you either cease and desist having invocations at the beginning of your meetings or I'm going to sue you." I looked him directly in the eye and I said, "Sue me." He went away, and he's yet to be heard from. We try to engage not only all of our Christian friends, but at times we'll have a Buddhist priest come in to pray with us, or the Rabbi will come in and pray with us, to encompass the diversity of religious influences that we have in our community. As you know, we have a Hindu temple and a Buddhist temple, and all these type of things. We do celebrate our diversity in Modesto. Not only ethnically but religiously. Obviously 99% of our people are Christians, so we think it's very important not only as an ongoing reminder to us of the religious significance as well as the roots we have. It also shows our community that we think this is a vital and important cog.

Q. So in general then, the City Council's attitude towards the Church of Modesto is very favorable.

A. Outstandingly favorable.

Q. What changes or improvements would you suggest that GMMA could make or that you would like to see? Are there any things that we could do as the Church of Modesto which would help the City of Modesto?

A. You know, that's a good question but a difficult one for me to answer. My immediate reaction is, I can't think of a thing because they have taken a very positive and high-level leadership role in bringing forward the Spirit to meet the spiritual needs of the people of our community. Anytime we felt their presence would be helpful, in the discussion or the creation of certain kinds of policies or whatever, they have responded in a most beautiful way. We have now kids at school who are part of the Church of Modesto that will come up to us when I am teaching and said, "Mayor, we want to pray for you and your family. What can we pray for?" I mean, you've got High School Seniors doing this, and Juniors and others, which is very impressive. The churches have moved into our schools in a very positive way. I know that's a delicate area for some schools. They do it in a very responsible way and I'm so glad to see that religious influence on the Campuses so they're available to the young people of Modesto.

But I think if you're going to have a dynamic, viable community, one of the key components is the spiritual one. Without that there's an emptiness and a void that cannot be replaced by any other. We can deal with the bricks and mortar and all those kinds of things, but we need people of the cloth who will come forward and assist us. I will tell you, in the twenty two years that I have been involved in local government, of course it's much more modern now and more effective, but we have always, always enjoyed the support of our spiritual community.

Q. You mentioned twenty two years. Do you see a difference between the influence of the churches in Modesto today from that of twenty two years ago?

A. Oh, they're much more active today.   In those days they had their small ministerial groups as some communities had, but the leadership of the Ministerial Association over the years has become much more active and in a positive way aggressive. I don't mean they're becoming an annoyance, but in a positive way have become very much a part of our community, beyond the Sunday services. That, of course, is critically important, and they are providing now extensive religious experience. Big Valley now will be expanding into a K-12 program on their campus. Calvary Temple has a good school. We have two high schools here, Central Catholic and Modesto Christian. All those things help in building the moral fiber of our community. With people who think like that, those attitudes are going to reflect in a very positive way as part of our community. But I'm glad to be part of a leadership team that has that kind of support.

Q. Would you like to share a story of how either the Lord or the church has impacted somebody's life or something close to you?

A. No question, and that's an easy one for me to answer. Over the years my wife has experienced a series of very difficult health problems. She has had two brain surgeries and a number of other health-related problems. Frequently when asked what can we pray for, and I've had pastors ask and we've prayed for various things, the first thing I ask them to pray for is my wife's health. We all have bridges to cross in life and one of ours has been that. I'm very, very pleased to say that as a result of that prayer and ongoing good medical care, her health now is as good as it's ever been. We feel part of that has been the continuing support through prayers that we received from thousands of people in our community.

I've had a lot of fun in the churches as well. I was out at Big Valley one day presenting the reconciliation [proclamations]. A kind of fun anecdote about Pastor Seifert. My wife and I have been married forty one years. The Pastor asked me in front of his very large congregation, "Mayor, to what do you attribute the success of your wonderful forty one years with your wife?" I said, "We made a pact early on that she would make the small decisions, but she would leave all the big decisions to me to make in our marriage. And I'm pleased to report, in forty one years we've never had a big decision to make." The congregation got a big kick out of that.

I wanted to tell you, both personally and as the Mayor of this City, how much Religion plays a role in our lives. Every decision that we make, whether it has direct impact on the churches or not, all the precepts of a high-level morality and to protect the spiritual privacy of our citizens, all those kinds of things, are constantly in our minds as we go about deliberating the business. I will tell you there's a lot of things that make a good Community, but the spiritual component, I always say, is the one that makes a great City even better.

D. A DEFINITION OF THE CHURCH OF MODESTO

The Church of Modesto (COM) is a group of churches comprised first and foremost by the churches existing within Stanislaus County, California, who share a belief system centered on the Deity of Jesus Christ and the inspired Scriptures. They are churches who have identified themselves as part of the Greater Modesto Ministerial Association (GMMA). It would also include all the churches in the same area who hold to a traditional Christian doctrine, but may not have formally joined the GMMA. Because they are members of the Body of Christ they are inherently members of the Church of Modesto, active or inactive. However, for the purpose of this study, when the COM is referred to, it is intended to mean the churches who actively participate in the GMMA. There is no official membership in the GMMA, and all involvement is completely voluntary. Churches' involvement vary at each activity.

The city of Modesto has a population of 179,770 people, with 419,000 residents in Stanislaus county. Modesto is the county seat. The city cites one hundred fifty five congregations of all religions. Looking at the ethnic Christian congregations is valuable in understanding the city of Modesto. It has been said that there are approximately forty different languages spoken in Modesto. The world is coming to our front door! There are about twenty two African-American congregations, twelve Hispanic, and twelve Asian. These numbers are subject to change but were obtained from church leaders in their respective ethnic communities of Modesto. The remainder of churches are predominantly white. The number of ethnic congregations represented on a regular basis at Wednesday pastor's prayer time is currently around ten and growing.

The GMMA mailing list includes churches in the entire county. It mails to 133 Bible-believing congregations. Because the number of active congregations does vary considerably from activity to activity, attendance is best measured at the Wednesday Pastor's prayer time. That meeting averages around eighty to one hundred participants coming from approximately thirty five different churches.

For the intent of this study, the Church of Modesto will refer to those churches which hold to the values enumerated by the Greater Modesto Ministerial Association and are involved in COM activities on a frequent basis.

The Purpose Statement of the GMMA reads:

"To exalt the Lord Jesus Christ by working together to build His Church and obey His Word, while recognizing our distinctives in the body of Christ."

The objectives of the GMMA are:

1. To demonstrate love and unity in Christ by praying together

2. To enrich and encourage ministry excellence

3. Friendship with accountability

4. Address moral and social issues of our Community

5. Manifest a personal commitment to scripture

The 1998 Steering Committee
includes the following pastors:

Pastor David J. Seifert, President,
Big Valley Grace Community

Pastor Ross Briles, Treasurer, Sherwood Bible

Pastor Charlie Crane, Greater True Light Baptist

Pastor Joel Richards, Secretary, LaLoma Grace Brethren

Pastor Ken Swett, Prayer Chairman, Modesto Foursquare

Pastor Jeff Kreiser, Media Coordinator,
Living Faith Community

Pastor Jim Benedict, Member at Large,
Prescott Evangelical Free

Pastor Wade Estes, Member at Large, First Baptist

Pastor Reynaldo Mora, Member at Large,
Centro Christiano Vino Nuevo

Pastor Jeff Norman, Member at Large, Modesto Covenant

Pastor Don Christensen, Member at Large,
Harvest Rock Church

Mr. Todd Hunnicutt, Coordinator,
Lighthouse Prayer Ministry

D. CALENDAR OF EVENTS

CHURCH OF MODESTO — Fifty Years of Ministry

1948 Billy Graham Crusade
1948 Modesto Union Gospel Mission Founded
1966 Mayor's Prayer Breakfast Instituted
1970 Church in the Park Beginning
1983 David Seifert Becomes Chairman of GMMA
1983 GMMA Creates New Purpose Statement
                                        and New Board
1983 Luis Palau Crusade at Modesto Junior College
1986 First Community Marriage Policy
1991 Community Marriage Policy Renewed
1994 First Pastors' Prayer Summit
1994 Weekly Pastors' Prayer Meeting Begins
1995 Promise Keepers "Wake Up Call" All City Event
1995 Second Pastors' Prayer Summit
1995 First Oakland Promise Keepers Conference
1995 First Calvary Temple (CT) Drama,
                        Heaven's Gates, Hell's Flames
1996 Third Pastors' Prayer Summit
1996 Meeting at the Track
1996 First COM City Wide Crusade (Speaker - Tom Trask)
1996 Burned Churches Relief Gift to Mississippi Churches
1996 Second Oakland Promise Keepers Conference
1996 *Heaven's Gates, Hell's Flames* (Second CT Drama)
1997 Fourth Pastors' Prayer Summit
1998 *Heaven's Gates, Hell's Flames* (Third CT Drama)
1997 COM Flood Relief Program
1997 First Fresno Promise Keepers Conference
1997 Second COM City Wide Crusade (Speaker-Tony Evans)
1998 Fifth Pastors' Prayer Summit
1998 *Heaven's Gates, Hell's Flames* (Fourth CT Drama)
1998 Pray Greater Modesto Crusade (Ed Silvoso)
1998 First Sacramento Promise Keepers Event

E. OBSERVATIONS

1. Before the 1980s, the churches in Modesto had much work ahead of them if they were to be termed the "Church of Modesto" (COM). They were better described as small kingdoms with high walls and very little communication.

2. The community leaders, specifically the Mayor and the City Council, recognize that the COM is a great asset to the city of Modesto.

3. Mayor Lang reports that other city mayors recognize and envy the cooperation between the GMMA and the Modesto city leaders.

4. Modesto's political arena has been impacted by the activism of the COM and through political victories by CLEAN, a grassroots political action organization.

5. In the Mayor's interview, he cited several impacts the COM has had on the city: the flood relief; the political victories of CLEAN; the pastors offering an invocation at each City Council meeting; the positive impact of the numerous christian schools within the community towards building the moral fiber of the community; and the number of vibrant churches in the community raising the overall moral atmosphere within Modesto.

SECTION ONE

PAST AS PREPARATION

"That the whole cause of schisms lies in sin I do not hold to be certain. I grant that no schisms is without sin but the one proposition does not necessarily follow the other. From your side Tetzel, from ours Henry III, were lost men: and if you like, Pope Leo from your side and from ours Luther (although from my own part I would pass on both a lighter sentence). But what would I think of your Thomas More or of our William Tyndale? All the writings of the one and all the writings of the other I have lately read right through. Both of them seem to me the most saintly of men and to have loved God with their whole heart: I am not worthy to undo the shoes of either of them. Nevertheless they disagree and (what racks and astounds me) their disagreement seems to me to spring not from their vices nor from their ignorance but rather from their virtues and the depths of their faith, so that the more they were at their best the more they were at variance. I believe the judgment of God on their dissension is more profoundly hidden than it appears to you to be: for His judgments are indeed an abyss." [4]

C.S. Lewis

Whenever anything of significance is accomplished there is always a time of preparation leading up to it. God prepared Israel to enter the promised land with forty years in the wilderness. Jesus prepared the disciples for their life ministry through a three year intensive discipleship period. In the case of the Church of Modesto it appears that one of the initial steps down the path of unity was via the 1948 Billy Graham Crusade. From that point to the first Pastors Prayer Summit in January of 1994 it appears that God was tilling the soil of unity in this community.

Some events which have contributed to unity were instigated by church leaders for the intended purpose of drawing the churches together. Other events were created or orchestrated by God Himself to push the churches in the direction of unity. Section one presents several interviews to show some of the incidents which God used to push Modesto in the direction of community wide church unity during that period.

Chapter 2

THE GREATER MODESTO
MINISTERIAL ASSOCIATION
AN EARLY HISTORY

A. THE MODESTO MANIFESTO - OCTOBER 1948

B ILLY GRAHAM describes his first evangelistic campaigns in his biography: *Just as I Am.* He writes:

> Following our first citywide Campaign in September 1947, in Grand Rapids, Michigan ... we held a number of others; but Augusta, Modesto, and Altoona now stand out in my mind for various reasons .... Modesto .... A large tent had been erected for the event. Right from the first, we were encouraged by the response. Some nights we had to turn hundreds of people away because of lack of space. Some of the Modesto leaders encouraged us to stretch the original two weeks into three. I had to decide against it, however, due to pressing responsibilities at Northwestern [Schools].

> But Modesto not only encouraged us to continue city-wide campaigns, it also provided the foundation for much of our future work in another way. From time to time Cliff, Bev, Grady, and I talked among ourselves about the recurring problems many evangelists seemed to have, and about the poor image so-called mass evangelism had in the eyes of many people. Sinclair Lewis's fictional character Elmer Gantry unquestionably had given traveling evangelists a bad name. To our sorrow, we knew some evangelists were not much better than Lewis's scornful caricature.

One afternoon I called the team together to discuss the problem. Then I asked them to go to their rooms for an hour and list all the problems they could think of that evangelists and evangelism encountered.

When they returned, the lists were remarkably similar, and in a short amount of time, we made a series of resolutions or commitments that would guide us in our future evangelistic work. In reality, it was more of an informal understanding among ourselves—a shared commitment to do all we could to uphold the Bible's standard of absolute integrity and purity for evangelists.

The first point on our combined list was money. Nearly all evangelists at that time—including us—were supported by love offerings taken at the meetings. The temptation to wring as much money as possible out of an audience, often with strong emotional appeals, was too great for some evangelists. In addition, there was little or no accountability for finances. It was a system that was easy to abuse—and led to the charge that evangelists were in it only for the money.

I had been drawing a salary from YFC [Youth For Christ] and turning all offerings from YFC meetings over to YFC committees, but my new independent efforts in citywide campaigns required separate finances. In Modesto we determined to do all we could to avoid financial abuses and to downplay the offering and depend as much as possible on money raised by the local committees in advance.

The second item on the list was the danger of sexual immorality. We all knew of evangelists who had fallen into immorality while separated from their families by travel. We pledged among ourselves to avoid any situation that would have even the appearance of compromise or suspicion. From that day on, I did not travel, meet, or eat alone with a woman other than my wife. We determined that the Apostle Paul's mandate to the young pastor Timothy would be ours as well: *"Flee . . . youthful lusts."* (2 Timothy 2:22, KJV).

Our third concern was the tendency of many evangelists to carry on their work apart from the local church, even to criticize local pastors and churches openly and scathingly. We were convinced, however, that this was not only counterproductive but also wrong from the Bible's standpoint.

We were determined to cooperate with all who would co-operate with us in the public proclamation of the Gospel, and avoid an antichurch or anticlergy attitude.

The fourth and final issue was publicity. The tendency among some evangelists was to exaggerate their successes or to claim higher attendance numbers than they really had. This likewise discredited evangelism and brought the whole enterprise under suspicion. It often made the press so suspicious of evangelists that they refused to take notice of their work. In Modesto we committed ourselves to integrity in our publicity and our reporting.

So much for the Modesto Manifesto, as Cliff called it in later years. In reality, it did not mark a radical departure for us; we had always held these principles. It did, however, settle in our hearts and minds, once and for all, the determination that integrity would be the hallmark of both our lives and our ministry. [5]

B. INTERVIEW WITH CLIFF BARROWS [6] OF THE BILLY GRAHAM EVANGELISTIC ASSOCIATION.

Q. Would you begin by telling where you grew up, and when you came to Christ.

A. The San Joaquin Valley, and the very heart of the Valley, Ceres and Modesto, are very special to me. If I could use the word precious, that might be appropriate. Peter used it quite a bit, so maybe I could use it too. My physical life began there, but my spiritual life began there as well. I gave my heart to Christ under the preaching of Dr. Carl Deerfelt down in Ceres when he was pastor of the First Baptist Church there. I was 11 years of age. That would have been in 1934.

My heart was open to the Savior, and I remember the message that he preached as if it were yesterday. He spoke from John 3:16 and had us place our name in the verse. I did. I realized that the Lord Jesus died on the cross for my sins, for the sins of Cliff, and it was because of God's love that He sent his Son. All I could do was respond when the pastor invited us to. I remember walking forward that morning. I was frightened to do so, and yet I knew I had to. I gave my hand to the pastor and my heart to the Savior. My life took on a new dimension, even in those young years, from that time on. Of course, I had a rich heritage and a mother and dad who loved the Lord. They were hard working farmers out there on Service Road. They lived a life of exemplary attitude and manner before us as children. It had a profound impact upon me.

Q.   How large was your family? How many children?

A.   There were five children. Of course two of them came along later in life. Three of us, myself and my two sisters, Mary Jean and Shirley, were the ones that lived together in the home out there in the country. In fact, Mary Jean is married to Ben Jennings, a former pastor of the Prescott Bible Church. I believe their daughter, Colleen, is married to one of your Pastors at Big Valley Grace, John Fraioli.

Under the teaching and the ministry of Dr. Deerfelt, and then later with Dr. Paul Jackson who became pastor of that church, my life really grew. A Christian service band was established in the church, encouraged and nurtured by Paul Jackson. Scores of young men and women went out into full-time Christian service, myself included. I went to Bob Jones College and when I left in 1940 I did not really return back to the area to live, except in the summer times, after that. I dedicated my life to full-time Christian service at Mt. Hermon during our summer conferences. That was the one thing we looked forward to even as young children. We had to work and earn our money to go because money was scarce. We'd save our pennies, nickels and dimes. We'd go to that week of conference at the family camp down in Redwood Circle at Mt. Hermon. A lot of that has changed now.

My friendships with the people in the area were developed in those early years. Lorne Sanny, who lived in Modesto, was a couple years older than I, but we became very good friends. I played the trombone, and we would hold meetings in the migrant camps for the workers. I would play and my sister, Mary Jean, hauled a little bill-horn peddle organ around with us. She would sit at the organ and play; I'd sing and play my trombone. Sometimes we'd sing a duet. Then Lorne would speak. We did that in front of a couple of taverns in town. We had street meetings as well during those days there in Modesto.

As I reflect on evangelism and the unity of the churches now that is taking place in that city, I just remembered that one of my first real impressions of what an evangelist was in those early, early days. It would have to be back close to the time of my conversion, maybe even before, when Porter Barrington came to the area. They sent up a tent, I believe it was. They had a crusade there in the area. But I was impacted then with a real desire to somehow be involved in evangelistic work or in the music of evangelism. That was in the early 30's. I set my heart to that after surrendering for full-time Christian service at a campfire in Mt. Hermon. Dick Hillis had the devotions and the teaching that week. When it came to surrender and to commitment for full-time service, I remember it so well, I reached down and picked up a little stick by the campfire and tossed it in, representing my life I'm giving now to the Lord.

Dick Hillis had a great impact upon me. I have happy remembrances of him and his dear wife, Ruth. His brother, Don, did as well, but it was through Dick's ministry that I dedicated my life to the Lord. He was one of the speakers at Mt. Hermon. That goes back many, many years ago.

Q.   Were the churches in a good place of cooperation? Or were they more into their own worlds at that time?

A.   I think they were pretty much into their own world. Aside from the name Billie Sunday, who never came to that area immediately, I don't know that they experienced or knew too much of a cooperative type of evangelism. Of course, I was very young. I didn't know anything about it myself. I knew that the Lord was blessing. There was more unity within the denominations. I know that our church was very close with the Grace Baptist Church in Modesto. It was in that fellowship that we went to Mt. Hermon and invited Dawson Trotman. It was from Dawson's ministry that Lorne went into the Navigators and that I went then to attend college back in Tennessee. We weren't aware of cross denominational unity. I don't think it was too much of an awareness of what could be done across those denominational lines. I do know that a few of the churches within their own denomination, like the Independent Baptists and the Regular Baptists, had some fellowship together and joint meetings once in a while. But that's as much of the unity that I was aware of.

Q. May we continue to talk a little bit about the Modesto Crusade?

A. I went away to Bob Jones [College] and graduated in 1944. I went to St. Paul, Minnesota, to be the Assistant Minister at the Temple Baptist Church. I was there for almost a year, not quite. Then I traveled with Jack Schuller, from down in Southern California, for a few months. It was in that context that I met Billy as a very young man in Winona Lake, Indiana, when Youth For Christ [YFC] was organized in 1944 and '45. It was in '45 that I was there. Soon after I was invited with my wife, Billie, by Torrie Johnson to join the Youth for Christ staff. Billy Graham was the first one that had been invited to do so and was their traveling evangelist. We teamed up then. That was 1945.

I became a full-time YFC associate in January, 1946. Then we continued under Youth For Christ for two years. Then Billy was appointed as acting president of Northwestern Schools in Minneapolis when Dr. W.B. Riley passed away. He took that responsibility, though it didn't keep him from traveling. He kept it until God would lead someone that would keep it in the right direction and was really committed to what Dr. Riley intended it should be, so he could turn it over to him. But in 1947, we wanted to go back to our home town areas and hold extended meetings.

Q. So the desire to return to your home towns was the motivation to do a crusade in Modesto?

A. We went to Charlotte first, which was his hometown, and we had a wonderful meeting. We extended it for a couple of weeks. That's written up in his book, *Just As I Am*. There is a little bit about Modesto. My father was very active in the Christian Businessmen's Association. His name was Charles A. Barrows. When the businessmen decided to sponsor the Crusades I inquired about going to my hometown. The men there were praying. This crusade was really born out of prayer. Pastors from different denominations were involved and we were invited to attend. Rex Humbard, Jr., came and set up the tent we used. We had sawdust on the floor, benches, and my grandfather made the pulpit. We still have it. The Crusade met at the five points on the end of McHenry Avenue. Ben Jennings was the director of Youth for Christ of Modesto. He was the chairman of the Crusade and helped coordinate the pastors. It was probably under the sponsorship of Youth for Christ.

It was during that meeting that we felt God was confirming on our hearts that He wanted us to thrust forth into evangelism. We had been in England in 1946, then Charlotte and now Modesto, and we felt God was uniting our hearts in the direction of evangelism. We were there, Grady Wilson, George Beverly Shea, Billy, and myself, having devotions every morning. Billy asked us to go back to our rooms and think about the pitfalls of evangelism and evangelists. He said, "Go make a list, then come back and we'll share our lists. We'll ask God to guard our hearts from the pitfalls on the list. Then we can really give our hearts to this ministry and protect the impact of the gospel we proclaim and keep our lives pure before Him." So we did that. We came back and there were four areas that we touched on. That is why we call this the Modesto Manifesto. God has honored our commitment to this standard. In fact, the Crusade and the Manifesto happened 50 years ago this autumn, 1948, in Modesto.

Q. Cliff, how did you sense the churches working together during that Crusade?

A. I felt that it was a great bringing together of the people. We had Beulah Covenant of Turlock and other significant churches became a part of that Crusade. We felt there was a real beginning of unity in a new way as a result of that Crusade. We did not have extensive follow up at that time, so I could not vouch for the aftermath.

As we came back to the Central Valley in following years, the people from the area supported other meetings, those in Sacramento, Oakland, San Francisco, and several up and down the Valley. There was a moving of God's Spirit in the Valley that was characteristic of what He was doing in the lives of individuals. Our Crusades were a part of that.

C. INTERVIEW WITH PETER JOHANSEN [7]

Q. Peter, please give a little of your background and how you are related to the Church of Modesto.

A. My folks moved between Empire and Waterford in 1920 when I was less than a year old. My mother had me in church all my life. We were farm people and I count it very fortunate that I grew up in a period when there was a serious depression. You had to raise your own food for there was not much money to buy things. I was born February 29, 1920. I have been in this county for a long time. My parents moved to Turlock and bought a farm. I attended a rural grammar school,

Former Modesto Mayor and Staff Pastor of First Baptist Church, Peter Johansen.

graduated from Turlock High School and then went to Modesto Junior College. My high school baseball coach got me a job that I had to work full time. Fortunately, I was selected to the executive training program and the company sent me to Cal. Berkeley. I worked a half day and they paid me a full salary, which was $18 a week. While there the professors came right into our place of business to teach the various courses.

Following that I went in the Army Air Corps in Fort Worth, Texas. While there, I headed up a high school and college ministry in a Christian church. I was a church member a long time before I came to Christ. It was then that I felt God calling me to go into the ministry. However, I had a wife and a child. When I came back to Modesto I went to work.

I felt that God called me to be active in the community and as a result I got involved. I was a founder of the Better Business Bureau here in Modesto, active in the Chamber of Commerce, President of the Merchant's Association, and even headed up all the Little League Baseball. I coached basketball and was very active in First Baptist Church, in all sorts of leadership roles.

Then I felt that God was calling me to serve in an elected position. I was appointed to the City Council and then elected to the City Council. I was later elected Mayor of the city. I served in city government from '57 to '67. I was Mayor from '63 to '67. During those years I was always active in the church. I headed up the college ministry at First Baptist Church for about nine years, which was a big ministry even back in the 60s with 150 to 200 kids.

I had a brother who in the 50s received Christ one Sunday. The following Wednesday he was stricken with polio. He was unconscious for fifty eight days. When he regained consciousness he couldn't talk or do anything. Being in an iron lung, the nurses communicated with him by writing upside down or backwards, and he would answer by blinking his eyes. The head nurse called me one time and said, "We've been working for a week. We cannot find out what this boy wants." He finally communicated that he wanted me, his brother, to pray with him. I had never prayed out loud with a member of my family at that point, but I started praying reading the Bible with him. Next, he wanted me to pray with everyone else in an iron lung, of which there where seven in Stanislaus County Hospital.

It was during this time when I reevaluated my life. I was a successful businessman and active in the community, but something was missing. I was having breakfast with a fellow once when the Sundial first opened. I said, "You know, I really would like to have the enthusiasm to share Christ with people the way you do." He simply asked me, "Peter, have you ever asked Jesus Christ to forgive your sins, come into your life and totally take over?" I said, "No, I've always been in the church." So at that point I invited Christ to come into my life and be Savior and Lord of my life. Almost immediately I had a zeal to share the Lord with others and I began to do that. I saw quite a few businessmen come to the Lord. Anytime someone would be in trouble, I began to talk with them and share the love of Christ with them. And of course, my life got exciting.

During this time when I was Mayor I had the joy of seeing the City Attorney and City Manager come to the Lord. I really felt God wanted me to continue impacting lives. About that time Campus Crusade came to Modesto and was holding an Evangelism Seminar at Orangeburg Avenue Baptist Church. I attended. This particular night I went late because I had a city council meeting. One of the leaders sat down beside me. After the presentation was finished he said, "Do you happen to know the Mayor or City Councilmen of this town?" I sheepishly said yes. He said, "Well, who are they? We would like to meet with the Mayor." I didn't know how to handle it but I said, "I am the Mayor of Modesto." He was shocked and surprised. To make a long story short, it wasn't long before I started teaching Evangelism for Campus Crusade all over California. Then Crusade started a church management course, so I taught that all over the U.S. and even outside the country with them. It was a five-day course. I didn't get any pay, but they paid my travel expenses. This was right at the end of being Mayor. Around 1966. I did not rerun for office in '67.

A turning point of my life was when I was asked by the Rotary to lead six men to Fiji, New Zealand, for nine weeks. It was during that tour that I really felt God calling me to get out of the business world and enter ministry full time. My business had been a retail flooring business. I sold that in 1970.

It was at that time that Pastor Bill Yaeger asked me to join the staff at First Baptist Church. I served on the church staff from 1970 until I retired in 1986. I've been retired over twelve years now, but I've always been active in the educational field in our county. I've headed up two different school bond drives and a bond override drive. The bond we passed paid to build about ten schools. Every time there was a new superintendent or a new president of the Junior College, I would try to go to them, tell them education was a priority, and I was available to help them. Schools called on me a number of times for various responsibilities.

You asked a little earlier about what I am doing today now that I'm retired. I was Chairman of the flood relief thing for the Church of Modesto. That was a real joy, to be able to help poor people.

About five years ago another fellow and I felt that we needed to get all people that used federal dollars together to begin to communicate together, to know what one another was doing. It was very painful the first year, but as a result of that I see now that city and county are getting together to occupy a building. I've seen more cooperation than I've ever seen in this county since I've lived here. The name of it is Pacific Agency Council.

About ten years ago I founded an organization called Stanislaus Partners in Education. We wanted to get the public more involved in education in the schools. We began to form partnerships between churches, service clubs, businesses, and schools. At this particular point we have somewhere between 125 to 150 partnerships. Just outstanding things are happening. We've been able to get major grants of money. We now have businesses helping write curriculum for the Junior College and Riverbank High School. Business and industry have actually been developing a school curriculum. Last year I heard about an organization that had been active in San Diego for ten years. They had been able to drop their Hispanic drop-out rate in high school by over 50% in ten years. Mike Keckler and I invited those people to come up and make a presentation here. In September of '97 we put that program into three schools. Basically, it is a nine-week course on parenting and how to be involved in the school.

And of course, I've been tutoring students at Kirschen school for the last five years. I tutor two boys at this particular time. I have two tickets for tonight's game that I'm taking to them when I'm finished talking to you so they can go to the Modesto A's.

I lead three different Bible study groups. On Tuesday mornings at 6:00 I have a group of eleven teachers at Johanson High School that meets until about 7:10 [am]. I have a Saturday morning men's group here. And then I have a Tuesday night home group here with First Baptist Church. I am able to keep busy in retired life.

Q.   As a pastor in the 70s and 80s, what was the ministerium like? Do you see any changes in it today?

A.   The ministerium was pleasant to attend. However, there were what I would describe as turf battles. You know, we believe in sprinkling them and you believe in dipping them. We believe in tongues and you don't. There were great differences with not a whole lot of unity.

There were various leaders during those years. Then fifteen or sixteen years ago Dave Seifert became the leader of the ministerium. There was quite a difference between conservative churches and liberal churches, not realizing the amount of things that we really had in common. I remember one of things First B [First Baptist Church] did in the 70s when we brought John Wesley White, who was a Billy Graham associate for a crusade. We invited all the churches that we could find on the mailing list to participate, but there was really pretty minimal participation.

After Dave took over we had another crusade, with Luis Palau, in 1983. I headed that crusade up. All of a sudden we were getting some churches who were wanting to participate and be part of it. We trained the counselors as to what they should do. We gave everybody assurance that the counseling referral would be to the church that brought them. That was maybe the first outward signs of unity beginning to take place. Luis Palau did a super job. That was over at the MJC [Modesto Junior College] stadium.

Prior to that in the 70s, we had two crusades at what was then Del Webb Field, and now called John Thurman Field. At one of those crusades we had 1,013 decisions in seven days. We sent counseling cards to a lot of churches and asked them to advise us as to what they could do with follow-up. A member of a church brought this person and they were with them. We at First B referred to that church. But then as we did follow up thirty days later, not many of the churches had even done one follow-up contact on the decision cards that were sent to them. Now that was First B doing the crusades. During the John Wesley White Crusade we didn't get a whole lot of churches working together either. But in 1983 with a community effort for the Luis Palau Crusade I began to see unity.

Q. In the 70s you had the Del Web Field Crusade where there was really no unity and 1,000 decision cards that dropped through the cracks. Then there was the John Wesley White Crusade with a little improvement. And in 1983 a third effort with the Luis Palau Crusade and some improvement on the churches working together and the beginning of a sense of unity. How did your ministry at First Baptist Church contribute to a sense of unity within the community?

A. I would say our Ministerium attendance, including mine, became more sporadic because a little discouragement set in. But then after the Palau Crusade and David Seifert became the leader, I saw unity beginning to raise it's head.

At First Baptist Church we began to have a local extension of seminary and as well as recommend that their people begin to attend classes. That was probably in the late 70s, early 80s where that spirit of unity was building. Then through the Institute of Church Imperatives [ICI] in the early 70s, there was very little local church participation. But by the late 70s, early 80s, local pastors were bringing some of their leaders to the ICI. There again the walls were coming down and a spirit of unity was beginning to build. I think ICI had a part in it as I saw many local pastors attend. I remember Pastor Ken Silva from River Oak Grace [Community Church] coming to evangelism training and getting evangelism started while he served at Big Valley Grace [Community Church].

Q. Who were the key people who played a part in your ministry?

A. Probably I have to go back first of all to my high school age in the 30s. There was a pastor by the name of Ivan Bell who was a pastor in Turlock. He had a tremendous influence on my life. He was the pastor for over fifty years at First Baptist of Turlock. As I was an adult I was being fed more by Navigators and Campus Crusade than by my local church. I was attending seminars, courses, conventions, and Navigators back in the 50s, crusades in the late 50s and early 60s. A lot of my spiritual growth, maturity and training were coming from Navigators. Unfortunately it wasn't coming from my local church. When I started the first men's Bible study at First Baptist [Church] in 1958, it was an early morning, 6:00, men's Bible study. I was called before the Board of Deacons for trying to ruin the Wednesday night prayer service. I don't want to demean the local churches, but I feel in many cases the parachurch organizations have provided the mechanism for spiritual growth in many peoples lives. Now in the last 20 years I see local churches doing that, you know teaching evangelism, discipleship and how to have a successful marriage. But I didn't see that in the 40s and 50s. Unfortunately, or factually, I think Campus Crusade and Navigators played an important part in my spiritual growth and development, and contributed to leadership training, which indirectly contributed to the unity here in Modesto. They were a part of the foundational work.

While I was on staff at First Baptist Church one key person was Pastor Yaeger, of course. He was an outstanding leader and I enjoyed and grew from his and Pastor Ron Blanc's teaching. They were both students of the Word.

Bud Lacore and I were very close. After Bud and I became Christians we had a Tuesday, early morning Bible study for about two years. Then Bud became a leader, and I went on to lead other men. Bud was just a super Christian and his life exhibited just a dramatic change. And yes, Bud did have an influence in our community to help bring about unity.

As we worked on the Marriage Policy, Jim Talley was a very important person in helping bring about unity in the churches of Modesto.

As I already mentioned, when Dave Seifert became the leader of the ministerium he was a very key person.

Q.   Had God done anything in your heart to prepare you for this movement of unity?

A. Actually, again it was Navigators and Campus Crusade who really were working to bring about the unity of the churches. They were teaching church management courses to all breeds and brands, and trying to bring about unity. Then Navigators were encouraging churches to do the things which they were doing: teaching discipleship, evangelism and how to lead Bible study groups. I saw churches around the state and the country beginning to work together a little bit more.

One thing that I think had something to do with unity in 1966 was the first Mayor's Prayer Breakfast. I met with six men every Monday night, mainly in my living room. We did Bible study and prayer. They became my advisory council for being Mayor. They became the committee that helped us start the first Mayor's Prayer Breakfast. At the breakfast we passed out decision cards with three responses on them. One of the responses was, "I would be willing to join a morning Bible study." To make a long story short, we had 320 men at that breakfast and seventy eight of them checked they would be interested in being in a Bible study. All of a sudden we had seventy eight men with no leaders. I agreed to lead four morning groups. Dr. Ben Jennings and myself actually wrote the studies. Dr. Merrill Alexander and John King from Turlock also agreed to lead a study. But those men were from all sorts of churches. I saw a movement here where men wanted to be in God's word with no concern about whether they were Catholic, Presbyterian, Baptist, or what.

Q. Following the 1948 Billy Graham Crusade,this appears to be the first substantial movement toward breaking down denominational walls here in Modesto.

A.   Within one year we expanded to one men's Bible study group in Oakdale, two in Turlock, one in Patterson, and fifteen here in Modesto. In order to raise up leaders I wrote A Leaders Training Guide, which later became First Baptist's Bible Study Leaders Training Guide.

Usually Pastor Ben Jennings, of Prescott Bible Church, and I met with leaders once a week to go over the lessons. Ben was a tremendous support to me during my years in public office. He prayed for me on a continual basis.

There was another step in 1969. Lee Davies was Mayor and we started the first Community Youth Prayer Breakfast. At that first prayer breakfast we had over 500 students. We had to work with the school systems in order to get them excused from school for an hour during first period. That became very interdenominational. There began to be much excitement in the youth area. I remember John Hogan who was president of the student body at MJC [Modesto Junior College]. He received Christ and then became a leader and willing to help us put on these breakfasts. However, after Mayor Davies there were people in the community who didn't think the Mayor's name should be used, so it was discontinued as a Mayor's Prayer Breakfast.

Q.   Would you share any supernatural experiences in which God demonstrated His handiwork in causing this movement?

A.   I would suppose that after the first youth breakfast I saw high school kids on drugs. Then our small group of men sponsored a music concert in Graceada Park where we gave an invitation to receive Christ. We had a lot of kids there on drugs. As a result of that we started, along with Dr. Jennings, the Church in the Park. We held Bible studies at Graceada Park. When winter came along in 1970, we needed a place to meet. We moved it to the House of Carpets. We started out with 100 kids there and soon grew to 250. We actually had kids giving and selling drugs to other kids who were coming to the study. The police and Sheriff's departments worked with us very closely. I saw God do many miracles in lives. Then it became such a chore that we could no longer handle it. We had a school teacher, named Wendell Woodthorpe, and Jim Talley take over the ministry. We worked with them, but we were business people and we couldn't put in thirty to fifty hours a week doing this ministry. This is where I first met Jim Talley. It's also where Dr. Jon Venema, of Western Seminary, gave his life to Christ. There's a number of people now in ministry that came to Christ through the mechanism of Church in the Park.

Most churches weren't ready for these types of kids. I remember going to a church with six kids; two kids had long hair, one had an earring, and one was bare-footed. The Church in the Park filled a void. Gradually as the Church in the Park was involved with churches, churches began to take an interest, especially First Baptist and their youth pastor, Bill Stewart. So I saw God's supernatural power working in miraculous way in kid's lives. After I went onto church staff in '70, I became less and less involved with the Church in the Park.

Q. Why do you think God chose to begin such a work in Modesto?

A. God wants to see this type of unity everywhere in the world. I really feel that God has already used Modesto as a bit of a model around the world. I'm excited, for instance, about the Lighthouses of Prayer. I thank God as we really unite in prayer as a group of Christians. Not Methodist or Baptist, but Christians. God is going to use that mightily. Prayer is so powerful. I think God wants us to bring about unity within denominations. I think Satan has used, over the years, denominations to his benefit. There are so many things that we have in common, no matter what our brand is, that we need to concentrate on the love of the Lord Jesus Christ and the love that God has for us.

I think as a result of some of the series of events that happened over thirty years, the leadership of the ministerium, and the unity developing in the ministerium, which I wasn't a part of because I was retired, this is where we need to have a model. I really feel strongly it's God's choosing.

Q. Can you think of any down sides to this movement of unity?

A. No. I can think of a little criticism though. I think its important the Modesto Ministerium reach out more to Catholic and women ministers than they have. I even think there are many things we have in common with the Jewish faith. We don't want anyone to feel left out. We can't have isolationism. I really feel that the Ministerium has to reach out to Catholic and women pastors. My criticism would be we haven't done it enough. We need to do it more.

Q. What lessons or principles have you observed here in Modesto which could help other communities bring their churches together?

A. It only takes a few really dedicated people to their community and to prayer to bring it about. You need key leaders dedicated to prayer, creating a vision that we want to bring unity to our community. It doesn't take fifty or even twenty churches, but a few people dedicated to prayer and seeking God's direction with a vision to bring about unity and action. Love requires action. If Christians really have love they're going to be moved to action to bring about unity.

D. OBSERVATIONS

1. Modesto's journey down the path of unity initially began in 1948 with the cooperation of churches on the Billy Graham Crusade. It has continued from that beginning with greater intensity in the past fifteen years. Unlike much of modern life, deep-rooted unity is not a quick process.

2. It appears that the Mayor's Prayer Breakfast was an early event which God used to till the soil of unity in Modesto in 1966, even though it was not conceived nor directed by any local church. Peter Johansen was serving as Mayor at that time.

3. A third early cooperative venture was the Church in the Park ministry to the counterculture in the early 70s. Though it involved only ten churches, it was a building block of unity. It produced the fruit of many changed lives who carried a new spirit into the churches. A spirit which placed a lower value on denominational walls and a higher value on reality of faith. One changed life springing from the Church in The Park was Dr. Jon Venema, Dean of Western Seminary's Sacramento campus.

4.   It only takes a few Christians who are fully dedicated to unity to begin the process. Peter Johansen was just such a man.

5.   Peter Johansen represents a Godly servant who sees the value he has to offer as a retired citizen. His vast leadership experience continues to benefit the city and especially the Church of Modesto. He serves as a great inspiration and role model to all who are approaching retirement years. Though not directly involved in the COM, his influence is felt just the same.

6.   Involving city leaders who are Christians in spiritual and church related events is strategic if the whole city is to be effected.

Chapter 3

Recent History of the
Greater Modesto Ministerial Association

A. INTRODUCTION

OVER THE PAST fifty years, Modesto has experienced numerous events which have contributed solidly toward community-wide church unity. A high percentage of those events have occurred since the Luis Palau Crusade of 1983, with a dramatic increase following the first Pastor's Prayer Summit in 1994. Frequently it seems that God works through key people. It's not simply a matter of the "right man at the right time," but more like "God's appointed man at God's appointed time."

After over fifteen interviews on the Church of Modesto, one point has been emphasized repeatedly: Dr. David Seifert is one of those "appointed men" for "God's appointed time." Much of the unity has been on David Seifert's "watch" as chairman of the Greater Modesto Ministerial Association (GMMA). By his own admission, he has desired to pass the torch on to someone else, only to have God impress on him that it was not time to leave the post yet.

Since his arrival in Modesto in 1977, God has blessed David's efforts and faithfulness in growing Big Valley Grace Community Church, a successful, "life giving," nondenominational church and Christian school. God has also blessed his faithful and humble, yet strong leadership of the GMMA since 1981.

B.   INTERVIEW WITH DR. DAVID SEIFERT [8]

The following interview is Dr. David Seifert's perspective on the Church of Modesto. This interview with Dr. Seifert was conducted in his office at Big Valley Grace Community Church on August 11, 1998:

Q.   Dr. Seifert, would you give a little of your background? How you're related to the Church of Modesto and a thumbnail sketch of your ministry.

A.   I've been in Modesto for over twenty one years now. In 1977 our family made the trek up [Highway] 99, having spent seven years in Southern California and before that [we were] back in the midwest. It was a major step, but I kept asking the Lord along the way to really confirm, to just reveal to me that hand of blessing would be on this venture. I remember getting somewhere on this side of the Fresno area, or maybe Bakersfield, in the big valley. Just sensing the hugeness of this valley, having studied it on a map and looking at this thing, you could put the whole land of Israel inside this valley. Just how much of our produce is grown here? Then I began driving by these grapevines. Just vineyard after vineyard driving up Highway 99. We spent a night with a family in Madera. I guess it was on the trip that I began to notice carefully the way these vines were structured. There was a solid, vertical post, with the vine growing up around that post, and then there would be wires that would run horizontal to the ground. There it was in the form of a cross. All I could think of was John 15:5, "I am the vine, you are the branches. He who abides in Me, and I in him, bares much fruit." We began to ask God as a family at that time for much fruit. That was a real desire.

For the first number of years in Modesto, I was not interested in joining any ministerial association. One man visited just a few months ago that knew me back when I first came. In fact he was a financial consultant of ours. He knew I wasn't interested in a ministerium at that time. He came up after our Wednesday noon time of prayer, and the first thing he said was, "David, you sure have changed." I think that's a good thing. That's not something we should be embarrassed about. We want to change. That's what this life is all about, to become more like our Lord.

I kind of got drafted into my role as chairman. That's neat as I look back on it now. At the time I didn't think it was so neat. I remember having attended the ministerium fellowship once or twice, which was weak. There were just a smattering of pastors that would attend, maybe a dozen. They were mainly the mainline denominations, and those which were not committed to the values of scripture that I was. Not all, but some of them.

A few years after I was here, in about 1981, I received a telephone call from Roy Blakely, who was one of the patriarchs of this area. Having built a strong Bible church, Roy asked if we would host the ministerium meeting. I agreed to do that. Eight pastors showed up. Four of them were on our staff, so it was just a small group. At the end of the meeting, Roy Blakely stood up and said, "It's time for us to elect a new president. I move we elect David Seifert. Do I have a second? All in favor say, aye. Any opposed?" Just like that. He had said nothing to me ahead of time. No mention of it. I could feel my neck getting red and the anger rising. I remember the conversation going on within myself as I believe I was listening to the Holy Spirit on the

The Greater Modesto Ministerial Association Leadership team. (Back row L to R) Rick Fritzmier, Wade Estes, Joel Richards, Todd Hunnicut, David Seifert. (Front L to R) Ross Bryles, Ken Swett, Charlie Crane, Don Christenson and Renaldo Morales.

issue of self-control. Then He kind of whispered to me, "David, don't blow your cool. You can send a letter and resign after the meeting." I graciously finished the meeting out. Before that day was over, the thought came to me, "Maybe I should pray about it." I prayed about it and a strange thing happened. I began to feel excitement. I believe it was prompted by the Lord.

To make a long story short, I called a meeting the next month and presented to them several things they would need to approve if I was going to be the president. They came back and approved them all. Basically what we approved was the Mission Statement for the GMMA and the basic Objectives of what our goals were. Our Mission Statement, or our purpose, was to exalt the Lord Jesus Christ by working together to build His church, and obey His word while recognizing our distinctives in the body of Christ. That has served us well these many years. We've seen no reason to re-address that. We had five Objectives: (1) to demonstrate love and unity in Christ by praying together; (2) to enrich and encourage ministry excellence; (3) friendship with accountability; (4) to address the moral and social issues of our community; and (5) to manifest a personal commitment to scripture. That has been our commitment. What we've done with that is to put them on every letter we send out so that any of those who think we ought to be doing something different can notice what our charter is all about. It seems to keep distractions down to a minimum. It has worked well to leave it right there.

Q.   Had God done anything in your heart to prepare you for this movement of unity?

A.   I think there were a number of things that God used. First of all I would say was the Prayer Summit. A time of spending four days together, without any agenda, just seeking God, was something extremely different and new to me. To do it with other pastors pastoring in the same community that I really did not know was a real heart changing time.

I remember that first Prayer Summit, this was back five years ago. After the facilitators from Northwest Renewal had left, we divided up into small groups. We were trying to figure what the Lord was telling us what to do next. As the groups began to report back in, the first group said they thought we ought to meet every week and pray together. I told them I thought that was nice, and wrote that on the board. Then the second group said they thought we should meet together weekly and pray. I said, "Whoa. That's interesting. Let's see what someone else has." Everybody had the same thing. My Lutheran friend, John Kruger, always liked to laugh. He said, "David, I enjoyed watching it finally dawn on your face that as the leader you would have to be there every week to pray." I struggled with that because I didn't have time for another meeting on a weekly basis. Yet now that prayer time has become absolutely vital, formative in our lives, and in our ministry. I think that has spun off and impacted our local church as well as many local churches.

Q. David, you have been leading the GMMA since 1981. Looking at it's history, what would you say was the turning point in the direction and momentum of GMMA?

A. There were a couple of turning points. One was the time when they embraced our Mission Statement and the clear objectives that we had, so we had a track to run on. We were purpose driven then. That would have been in '81 or '82. We did it immediately after I became chairman.

Then I also said, "Now, allow me to pick the Steering Committee, and I will pick them from a consortium of churches." Of course, they said fine, if you can get anybody to serve, go ahead. I think we started with about seven pastors, and now there's a few more, twelve or thirteen. That was the real turning point. We got organized with a Mission Statement, with basic Objectives, with an initial Steering Committee, and then with regular meetings.

I think the second turning point came on the first year of our Prayer Summits. About a year before that Prayer Summit, I had come to a personal crossroads. I had become disenchanted with what we were doing. We had great programs, and had a good number turning out. On a comparative level, I suppose it was an outstanding ministerium, but I had asked the Lord to give us more. I wanted to try and figure out who could take my place. I wanted out. As I would ask the Steering Committee members, will you take it? They all felt they couldn't lead it like they felt I was leading. Of course, if the truth is known, my secretary Frances Skiles, is the real key. She's the one who gets a lot of this stuff done. As I prayed about it, I just sensed from the Lord this strange, quiet message. I got a picture in my mind of a soldier on duty. The response I got from God was, "David, stay at your post. Just be faithful and stay at your post. Don't go AWOL." I said, "All right, Lord. We'll just keep going." Shortly after that I told the Lord, "Lord, you've got to do something." Then the Prayer Summit came. That was in January of 1994.

At that first Prayer Summit when the facilitators were walking away, I realized God had come and had spoken to us. He had dealt with us according to His agenda, and we would never be the same. I ran after the guys, you know, it was a very emotional time

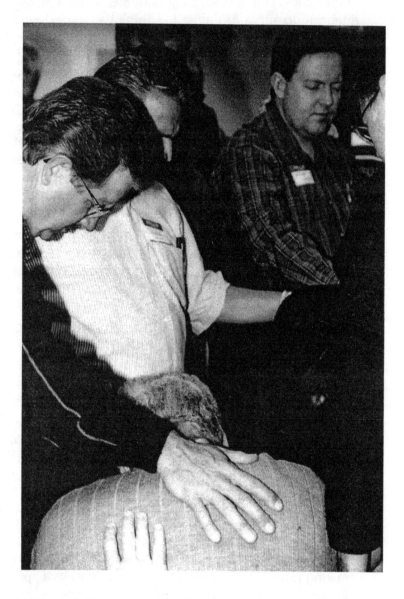

Praying for one another is a regular venue at Wednesday Pastor's Prayer Time.

for me. I just said, "Thank you." I had tears running down my face and I realized that God had answered my prayer. We would now be lead into some new, uncharted territory.

Then we started meeting every week for prayer. I think the first year ['95] we averaged about twenty five to thirty. We met fifty of the fifty two weeks. The next year ['96] we met every week and we averaged forty five. The following year ['97] we averaged about fifty five. So there has just been slow, steady growth. Now we run anywhere from sixty on a low time to 100 or more on a Wednesday. People, of course, visit from all over. Really that's just an hour to seek the Lord.

I think another thing that God did to prepare our hearts and to prepare me personally for this move- ment of unity was what I experienced at the Clergy Promise Keepers Conference back in Atlanta. Seeing that breaking up of men's hearts, of black and white, red and yellow, hugging each other in Christ and seek- ing forgiveness really moved me. That was a power- ful, powerful thing. I have not lived with a sense of racial discrimination or prejudice in my life, and I really wasn't aware of what those of the darker hue experi- enced in terms of suffering. I think that began to open my mind and heart in a major way. We just proceeded on.

Q. Were there any benchmark events in the GMMA which contributed to the unity in Modesto?

A. There were other things that happened locally. There were some Christian rallies that we did here. There were the Church of Modesto rallies. But probably for me one of the greatest events would certainly have been when we went to the Clergy Promise Keepers Conference. That was a bench mark. I think we had thirty five to forty of Modesto's pastors there. That was a bench mark because we brought the spirit of the conference back with us.

Another bench mark was the Oakland Promise Keepers. I don't know what year it was, but Modesto had thousands of men there. That was where we introduced the Church of Modesto tee-shirt for the first time. Just like the Church of Rome, the Church of Galatia, and Church of Ephesus, there is one Church of Modesto. It's composed of those who really know Christ. We began then to see ourselves as associate pastors of the Church of Modesto. I think that was the real turning point. Then we came home from that and we had a Church of Modesto rally right here in Modesto with about eight to nine thousand people. In fact, our newspaper even wrote a very good article about breaking down barriers, bringing people together. We took up an offering for three burned out, black churches in Mississippi. That was a turning point as well.

Another bench mark or another turning point, would be the recent prayer evangelism thrust. Let me just share how that happened. We were considering the possibility of an area-wide evangelistic crusade. We had been through a crusade in 1983 with Luis Palau.

We felt we had to evaluate it as well as listen to the Lord in terms of the cost, the resources, the energy, and the results. What kind of results do you really have from a crusade that ends up billing the local church? As we were discerning this whole thing, one of the pastors from the area came in with a recommendation of a crusade that he would like to come. This would have been 1997. So I asked him if he would chair the committee. We put about four guys on the committee from the Steering Committee. I said, "Now there's only one requirement. You have to come back with a united recommendation. You have to be together. Whatever that is, you have to say, 'We believe this is of God,' in your recommendation of the Steering Committee." They came back, and their recommendation was that they were not united and that they didn't have peace about moving forward. That was fascinating because of all the questions we had about the crusade: the finances, the results, and how it really builds the local church. Of course, we knew people would come to Christ, and that's what we wanted. As I closed that Steering Committee meeting in prayer, I said, "Lord, what do You want us to do? Here we stand, ready and available. We really need your direction." We had mixed emotions. How do we turn down doing a crusade and bringing people to Christ? But we did!

It was about three days later that we received a phone call from Ed Silvoso. Ed told us that while he was in Argentina, all he could think of was the Church of Modesto in the United States of America. That city needs to learn about prayer evangelism. He was coming to the States and we had a real quick meeting with about four of us from the Steering Committee. We just felt that God had put this thing together.

We began the process of prayer evangelism and all that it has entailed. We did a Sunday morning simulcast with fifty five or so churches. We prayer walked neighborhoods, helped people take responsibility for their spheres of influence whether it be the marketplace or school or especially their neighborhoods, and challenged them to put up lighthouse prayer placards in their windows. Now we've kind of moved from prayer evangelism, or "Pray Greater Modesto" as we called it, to "Lighthouses of Prayer".

Let me add something else, in terms of preparing hearts. He used prayer primarily to prepare us. That really needs to be emphasized. From time to time we would use a prayer guide. Like we went through Ted Haggard's book, *Primary Purpose*. That was a very powerful time where we were able to recognize our charismatic differences among the evangelical crowd. We were able to support each other on the big issues. We understood what the core values were and what some of the secondary issues were. When we're together we were going to focus on Jesus Christ, salvation, and His Word. That book helped us as we prayed together. Now we're just starting another one, *Fresh Wind, Fresh Fire*, by Jim Cymbala of Brooklyn Tabernacle. It's about what happens when God's Spirit invades the hearts of His people. We'll be working through that, reading it together. One of the things studying and praying through a book does is help bring your minds together because you're reading what God is doing somewhere else. You're studying through some principles related to prayer, you're praying about it, and that brings you together.

I think another great issue right now that we have ahead of us is the Westside Project. We're asking God whether or not we should move ahead to embark on building a youth center in the Westside. It will be used primarily by the churches in the Westside. In other words, it will be churches on the north, the east, the west, and on the south that will all work together to build this community project. That's a major undertaking, but we're in times of prayer and communication. We're going to discern on September 23 whether indeed that is what God wants us to do.

I think another of the supernatural experiences that the Lord gave us was at the Prayer Summit in January of 1997. While we were up in the mountains praying, it was raining in Modesto. It was not that the rain did something, but the floods. They had to release water because of the snow runoff. The floods that devastated areas of our community were so powerful. We were so concerned, wondering if we ought to come home. Yet we realized that we were to stay right there. Through that God really worked in a great way. Because it was one of the first projects that we had to pull together to accomplish. We put together "GMAC" as we called it, the Greater Modesto Area Churches Task Force. We went out to hire a well known executive in our community to head this task force up for up to a year. He, Tom Van Gronigen, ended up volunteering his time. He built a tremendous team. I think there were well over 200 homes that were repaired. Yes, some amazing things happened! That was a supernatural experience as well.

One more obvious supernatural experience was the thousands of people that have come to know Christ through the drama *Heaven's Gates, Hell's Flames*. That really was an amazing thing. Why that happened here and hasn't happened everywhere they go, I can't answer. Maybe it is because the pastors are covering the city in prayer and asking God to send revival. It came, and that's what we prayed for.

Q. Why do you think God chose to begin such a work of unity in Modesto?

A. I remember reading that Modesto was ranked about 297, or something like that, out of 300 of the favorable places to live in the United States of America. As we looked at that, we realized that, "Boy, if that's what the world thinks, I wonder what God thinks." Of course the name, Modesto, in Spanish means "humility," it means "humble." We were reminded of First Corinthians 1:27. It says, "God has chosen the foolish things of the world to put to shame the wise. God has chosen the weak things of the world to put to shame the things which are mighty. And the base things of the world and the things which are despised, God has chosen. And the things which are not to bring to nothing the things that are. That no flesh should glory in its presence." I think the Bible answers that God chose a humble place. I mean, Bethlehem was a humble place. Mary was a humble girl. King David, a little shepherd boy. I think that's God's way of doing things. He chooses those that don't think they're so great, and maybe that allows Him to get the glory and to do His works. I think that's one of the reasons he chose to do this in Modesto.

Q. Do you see any down side to this kind of community-wide church unity?

A. I think there can be a downside to it if you do not allow people the freedom to be who they are. I think you can very easily develop an in-crowd and an out-crowd. You can have expectations of pastors in your community becoming a part of something like this. Now, it can be your desire and you can desire that pastors be a part of it. You can pray for them. You can reach out and love them. You can invite them. You should do all of those things and befriend them, but I don't think you can expect them to come in the sense that you put pressure on them if they don't. I think you need to keep saying to yourself, and it's a little bit like *Romans* fourteen says, "How can I judge the servant of another?" If this man answers to the Lord of the church and he's not coming, who gave me the right to be his judge or to criticize him? The answer is that I don't have that right. My job is to bless him, to speak peace to him, to love him, to serve him, and to share with him. He is a brother in Christ. If he is, then we're together regardless of whether he comes to the meetings or the time of prayer or not. I think that's been a little bit of a point in tension, but I think basically we have walked that road and we have demonstrated unconditional love. You're not loved just because you come to prayer on Wednesdays, or just because you participate in prayer evangelism. No, I think our roll is to love all of the pastors. Even all of those who may be detractors.

There are some in our community who certainly are not on the same page, or should I say in the same book, that we are. I mean, they just seem to get their marching orders from a different book other than the Bible, or they have a real different view of it than what we have, and that is a very high view of scripture. God loves them. Christ died for all men, and we are to love them. It doesn't mean that we're going to steer away from our objectives. No, we have our Mission Statement. We have our sense of calling, and we would love for them to be included as they can. However, we find that those who do not have the same kind of fervor and perhaps personal relationship with Christ find it difficult to be our prayer mates because we come to meet the Lord. For some people, even some in the "ministry," that can be an uncomfortable place to be. But our goal has always been to love and to include them.

For a while it was kind of men only. Now we've got some women coming. We've never told the ladies that they couldn't come. We just recognize that, especially in a Prayer Summit where you have four days, that the men are going to share things that they won't share if there's women in the group. Now, in our weekly prayer meeting in the middle of the city, the women can cluster together as the men cluster together in small groups, and it works out fine. We don't want to be exclusive; we want to be inclusive. Yet we're following what the Lord wants us to do.

I think one of the critical passages that needs to be developed is Psalm 133:1, "Behold, how good and how pleasant, how sweet it is when brothers dwell together in unity." That Psalm goes on to say that it's like the dew coming off of Mt. Hermon. When you've been to Israel, there's a number of things that strike you. One is Mt. Hermon. It is nearly 10,000 feet high, and seated right there above where the Jordan River starts. If you stop and think about it, the clouds of precipitation and the fog come in from the Mediterranean, they hit that high mountain and condense into precipitation. It rains, the dew runs down, the head waters of the Jordan River begin, and it gives life to the entire nation–that one mountain. It's fascinating when you begin to understand that fact. And God says it's like the dew off of Mt. Hermon when brothers and sisters dwell together in unity. There is a blessing just like Mt. Hermon is for the entire nation of Israel. God says, "There I will command my blessing."

I want to add that it's not easy to maintain unity. Paul says we need to strive. We need to be diligent, to move fast and work hard to create the unity, and to maintain what we have in Christ.

Q. What lessons or principles have we observed here in Modesto which could help other communities bring their churches together?

A. Obviously, It all begins on our knees. The church moves forward on its knees. When a handful of people will really seek God together, then God acts. Second Chronicles 7:14, "If my people who are called by my name, will humble themselves and pray." That's our first response, whether it's a small group or whatever, just to pray, and to keep praying. Then to pray God's blessing, to learn how to pray a blessing like Numbers 6:24-26 instructs Israel to do. The words of Jesus in *Luke* six, how we're to bless our enemies. You begin praying God's blessing upon fellow pastors, and you begin loving them and reaching out to them. I think you need to lay everything you do before the Master. I think that's an important thing.

Also, we've learned how to set aside our agendas. We are so good at accomplishing programs and agendas that we still wrestle with the fact that don't we have to do something. We are doing something, we're praying. We are giving God glory. We are coming to seek His face. We are declaring how dependent we are upon Him. We are giving Him praise and honor. If He chooses to call us to do something, that's secondary. That has been a very hard principle to learn that the real act of doing is prayer. It is not what we do after we pray.

Now, God has lead us to do many things because we have prayed together and because God has brought unity, but I remember the words of Jesus. He prayed we would be unified so that the world would believe that God had sent Him. That He was really the Son of God. You know, as we love one another, then the world knows we must be disciples of His. Really, evangelism needs to come out ultimately of what happens. I think we need to see God's face, but then we need to see His hand. His hand is where He works. Once He turns His face toward us, we don't want His back toward us. We want His face toward us. *Numbers* six — the great blessing. But then He'll always lead us to be involved where His hand is working. God's hand is always working in evangelism, reaching the lost and building up Christians.

C. OBSERVATIONS

1. God anointed and appointed a leader for His work in Modesto. Dr. Seifert's fifteen years of leadership have provided stability as well as a vision for unity which is essential for a deep and lasting unity to be realized. This is not to say a community without a strong charismatic leader could not achieve unity, only that this was the path God led Modesto down.

2. The individual churches in Modesto were willing to defer their own personal agendas to a secondary position for the greater needs of the city as a whole.

3.   The heart of God is for the lost. Therefore the understood motive behind a unity focus must also be evangelism.

4.   Three key turning points for the Modesto Ministerium appear to have been: first, when Dr. Seifert became chairman and a Steering Committee was appointed (strong yet humble leadership is crucial); second, when the Mission Statement was drafted which coincided with Dr. Seifert's beginning as chairman; and third, when the first Prayer Summit was scheduled.

5.   Praying for fellow pastors and their churches changes the hearts of those who pray, and cultivates a heart for unity.

6.   The act of praying is what God desires from his churches and shepherds. Our programs are not what attracts His attention, but our prayers. If we seek to unite our communities, we must first draw near to God together in prayer.

7.   In addition to seeking God's face through prayer, we must look for His hand as we wait on Him. Once we identify where His hand is working, we must follow His lead to that place. He will lead His church to a place where He is already working. For Modesto, that has been in the area of unity within the Body of Christ.

SECTION TWO

PRAYER AS A FOUNDATION

"Disputations do more to aggravate schism than to heal it: united action, prayer, fortitude and (should God so will) united deaths for Christ — these will make us one". [9]

C.S. Lewis

"When did the Church of Modesto begin to experience great strides in unity?"

This is a common question from people who desire a similar work of God in their own communities. Many of the Modesto pastors would point to the first Prayer Summit. This was a time when God touched their hearts in an unmistakable and irreversible manner. That Prayer Summit birthed the Wednesday prayer meetings. That prayer time in turn, was the place in which God moved the hearts of the pastors to initiate the Pray Greater Modesto/Lighthouses of Prayer crusade.

Prayer became the foundation of Modesto's unity movement, just as prayer has always been the first step of any moving of God's Spirit. As C.S. Lewis reminds us:

"... *prayer ... will make us one.*"

Section Two presents four interviews describing the different aspects of prayer as a foundation for Modesto's unity.

Chapter 4

PRAYER SUMMITS

A. INTRODUCTION

On ONE TYPICAL cold and foggy January Monday morning in 1994, fifty very ordinary Modesto pastors loaded onto an average, not-so-comfortable sixty passenger tour bus. They headed off for a life-changing three-day Prayer Summit in the Santa Cruz Mountains. That experience appears to have changed not only their lives, but the course of their churches, their community, and maybe the world. This chapter is an interview with Ross Briles, Pastor of Sherwood Bible Church. Ross has attended each of the five Pastor's Prayer Summits to date. Ross lives out his Christian faith as a committed husband, father, pastor, and businessman. He also serves as Treasurer of the GMMA.

B. INTERVIEW WITH PASTOR ROSS BRILES [10]

Q. Ross would you please give a little of your own personal background and how you are related to the Church of Modesto.

A. I am the pastor of Sherwood Bible Church. I have been the pastor there since 1962. I have served on the Ministerium since 1983, and as it's Treasurer since 1986. I also am a businessman in town. I own Putt-Putt-Golf on Coffee Road. God has allowed me to be in both business and ministry most of my life.

Bob Cryder (L) and Ross Bryles, standing at the entrance of the Old Oak Ranch during a Prayer Summit. Bob has facilitated 82 prayer summits and three of Modesto's six, and heads a ministry designed to support local churches (see appendix).

Let me talk about the Prayer Summits. We've had five Prayer Summits now, with the first in 1994. To try to understand them, we need to go back several years prior to that first one. As a Steering Committee in the early '90s or late '80s, we felt it was important that the pastors pray together. We began trying to encourage that. Over a period of three, or even four, years the Committee tried to encourage this. We would set up times for one central location, and that didn't work. We did satellite locations so ministers wouldn't have to travel very far. Again we tried to do it at noon. We found that if you didn't offer a meal to go with it, it didn't work too well.

The focus, as we know today, grew out of a little bit of frustration from trying to get pastors to pray. That's not criticism, it's just a statement of fact. We weren't doing it. There would be at any of those efforts maybe eight or ten people. Normally it would be three or four people, often the staff of the host church. It was out of this frustration of trying to get the pastors to pray that we began to hear of the Prayer Summit Ministry out of Northwest Renewal Ministries and Multnomah College. We contacted them and set it up, deciding to do it the first week of the new year.

A little aside, before beginning the Prayer Summits, I had traditionally set aside that first week of the new year to go snow skiing in Colorado. That was one of the personal hurdles I had to get over. I haven't been back to Colorado snow skiing since then.

We scheduled it, but there were a few concerns I had. Number one, I didn't look forward to four days away from my vehicle. Going without my wheels is something that isn't exciting. Secondly, I wasn't sure how I was going to interact with professional clergy for four days. Thirdly, I wasn't sure what we were going to be doing. All those unknowns were kind of rolling around in my mind as we got on the bus and headed to the first Prayer Summit. It was at Mission Springs Camp, in the Santa Cruz Mountains.

We got on the bus, not really knowing what to expect. I think the best way for me to summarize how I felt was we were all in a circling mode. We circled one another, but we really never got to know one another. We asked all the normal questions and gave all the normal answers. But as we got to Mission Springs this began to break down.

I was assigned a room. The man who became my roommate was Charlie Crane. He drove over after the bus had arrived. I had known Charlie for a number of years, and Charlie is a good brother. We had a good opportunity to be together as roommates in that first Prayer Summit. In fact, it's rather interesting how the Lord has orchestrated different roommates over the years. I've never had the same one twice. I don't know whether that says something about me or against me.

We began that first year at the Prayer Summit not really knowing what to expect. I'll never forget the first thing they said to do. It was after we had lunch and had met briefly. They said, "We think you need to just go get alone. If necessary, just go take a nap." That was kind of an unheard of thing for me–not that I'm opposed to naps–but it was timely.

We now have had our fifth Prayer Summit. They have all been a little different, and yet one focus. But there are two things I remember from that very first Prayer Summit which I will probably never forget. While we were rejoicing and thanking God for what He was doing, one of the facilitators, Bob Crider, said, "As ministers we have become so good at what we do, it almost looks like God did it. But God never got west of Montana." I've never forgotten that.

The other word of wisdom and counsel from the facilitators in that first Prayer Summit was as we were preparing to leave. Being the type of personalities we pastors are, we felt we had to go back with something to do. One of the things we thought we ought to do is really get united. One of the facilitators said, "Gentlemen, don't go back to Modesto and seek unity. Go back to Modesto and seek Jesus. Because if you go back and seek unity, you may very well miss Jesus. If you go back and seek Jesus, you will find unity." We did come back to Modesto doing that very thing. The sense of unity has not grown out of seeking unity, because in doing that you have to figure out who has to give up what. Our unity grew out of sense of seeking the Lord, drawing closer to Him. An illustration I can give is one used in marriage counselling. How do two people, a husband and wife, draw closer together, as with a triangle illustration. As they move collectively closer towards the apex, Jesus, the distance between them diminishes.

Q.   In summary, a Prayer Summit is a four-day event when the pastors gather in a neutral location, in our case Mission Springs and now more recently at Old Oak Ranch in Columbia. There are no agendas, only to pray and to draw closer to the Lord. During the Summit we pray in large groups, in small groups, as individuals, and even have periods alone with the Lord. We do a lot of singing and praising God with no agenda other than to draw closer to Him. Is that correct?

A.   That's correct. It's a little hard to explain and I've tried to explain this to different people at different times. Part of the Prayer Summit is not just doing all of that. Part of it is just being quiet. It's a little hard for us pastors to be quiet before the Lord.

Another thing which grew out of the first Prayer Summit that I think has brought us to where we are today is a discussion of what we should do. We felt like we ought to pray together. We discussed how often. Once a month didn't seem to be enough and once every other week was a little bit awkward, trying to remember which week was the correct one. Finally we decided to pray every week. I for one thought it was a great idea, but I was not sure we could pull it off. We're now going into our fifth year. The Lord has helped it grow from a beginning of twenty or thirty guys, to now sometimes over a hundred.

Q. How did the Prayer Summits contribute to the great sense of unity that the Church of Modesto is experiencing today?

A. They brought us together for an extended period of time. You don't trust people you don't know. It gave us an opportunity to know one another away from our professional responsibilities, those professional responsibilities we are very protective of. I don't know of anytime that ministers are going to spend, even within their local churches, four days without some kind of an agenda. We just spent time. That spending time is actually essential and difficult to do.

Q. You mentioned also the Wednesday prayer time that grew out of it. Is it an extension of the Prayer Summits?

A. That's correct, Jim. Literally, we've now spent hundreds of hours together, not only at the Prayer Summits, but here in the city on Wednesdays for prayer time. I think most of us now plan our schedules around Wednesday. If I'm going to make a trip, I do my best to make sure I leave after Wednesday and be back before the following Wednesday. If I have to miss something, I'll miss Sunday in the pulpit as opposed to missing Wednesday prayer time.

Q. Speaking as a member of a multi-staff church, being with other pastors on Wednesday is great, but I am with other pastors all week long. Many of the pastors in smaller churches don't have a staff to work with. My sense is they may feel alone much of the time, so Wednesday provides them a team support.

A. That's true. I'm a single-staff church. As a result of that I would have to honestly say that there were many, many years I did not have anybody I felt like I could even talk to. I've been in Modesto almost thirty six years now. Today I could give you names of fifty guys I would feel comfortable sitting down and sharing with. For example, at the end of Wednesday's prayer time a few weeks ago one of the guys said, "Hey Ross, you want to have a cup of coffee?" I've known the guy for years, so I went to meet him for coffee. As we were drinking coffee, he said, "Ross, how are you doing?" Not the general how are you doing, but more specifically how are you really doing? We spent the next hour just interacting. I think that's the type of relationship that is awfully hard to come by in any quarters, much less in a pastoral quarters because we're the ones who are supposed to have all the answers. If we show any weakness or vulnerability, we sometimes seem to be attacked. I don't sense that as being where we are now. The Wednesday pastors' meeting is a real place of support and acceptance.

Q.   Had God done anything in your heart to prepare you for this movement of unity? As you were giving a little background on the Church of Modesto Ministerium, you said the that God had placed a sense of need in your heart. How was that?

A.   The reason Pastor Roy Blakely got involved with it is because the Modesto Ministerial Association had dwindled down to what many Ministerial Associations boil down to: people really don't come. Pastor Tom Foster, who was at St. Paul's Episcopal Church, had called Roy and told him that if he didn't do something with it, they were just going to give it a dignified burial. Pastor Roy agreed to do it, if he could get a bunch of guys to commit to coming. He called a bunch of us, and for the next nine months I tried to be there every time out of respect for Roy. At the end of that year Pastor David was elected by the old Sunday school way. Being put into a position where you couldn't gracefully say no. We thought he would write a letter of "I'm sorry I can't serve, I'd love to, but I can't." A week or so later God spoke to his heart. We are now thirteen to fourteen years into this thing. Pastor David is still the servant leader God has uniquely placed here. I think that's an important thing to understand. This would not have happened in other situations because, number one, busy people don't like to take on additional responsibilities. Secondly, there would not be the affirmation or the confirmation of his leadership, or anyone's leadership, in a normal situation. With God's timing, God gave the people with the gifts and abilities needed, and also gave the acceptance by the body as a whole.

This is an aside. There are some people who are rather concerned that we don't have annual elections. I don't sense that is what God wants. There have been people who have come on the Steering Committee, people who have gone off the Steering Committee over the years, and there's never been a problem. I think any of us would be willing to step aside at the moment we sensed that's what was wanted or needed.

God was doing some things in my heart to make me even willing to be around preachers very much. For much of my life before Prayer Summits I would rather be with a contractor than with a clergyman. Not that I had anything against clergymen, but I had more in common with a contractor. God had to do something in my heart to make me willing to be around preachers. He has continued to do that.

Q. Were there any bench mark events or statistics with the Prayer Summits that contributed to the Church of Modesto? I think that probably looking at the attendance over the past four years, how it has grown?

A. Yes, in round numbers, the first year we had mid 50s, the second year mid 60s, the third year mid 70's, the fourth year we were up in the mid 80s or low 90s, and in the fifth year we were again in that low ninety area. I can't say this from first-hand knowledge, but I've been told that the Church of Modesto Pastors' Prayer Summits are a little bit unique. Many others have begun at a higher level, maybe level off, then drop in numbers in subsequent years. The Modesto one is unique from the standpoint that we have grown, not by humongous numbers, but certainly have grown consistently over the years. There was a reason we experienced a leveling of attendance this last year. We actually had more registered, but there was an epidemic of flu and sickness that canceled out a number of people.

Another thing I think is important, and maybe this isn't the place to put it in but I'll throw it in anyway, is that some churches I have become acquainted with in other communities have scheduled Prayer Summits. Then thought they could do their own. When they launch out it just becomes an absolute disaster. I think the objectivity of someone outside of the community, who doesn't have an axe to grind and isn't trying to build a name for themselves, comes in with a stated commitment to listen to God. I think that's very important. I would never suggest we try to do it ourselves. We do a lot of the groundwork ourselves, a lot of the support work ourselves, and reaching out ourselves, but as far as facilitating it, I think you need somebody whom God has called to do this type of thing. It may not be Northwest Renewal. It may be somebody else, but I think is an important ingredient.

Q.   Would you share any supernatural experiences in which God demonstrated His handiwork in causing this movement even in your heart?

A.   This is a story that is sometimes difficult to talk about because it involves me. It's always interesting, I said earlier, who God orchestrates to be your roommate at Pastors' Prayer Summits. My first roommate was Charlie Crane, our African-American pastor brother. The second one was David Tan, who is from Singapore, a Chinese brother. Then I had one situation where I arrived, went to my room to put my stuff in my room, and nobody was there. I thought it would be interesting to see who God had in mind for me that year. I left, then went back so to see if anyone was there. I did have a roommate by that time, and it was kind of interesting. My roommate was a guy I knew and had talked to on numerous occasions. It was the only guy there I really had any hard feelings toward in any church in the city. God had placed this guy in my room. As I look back on it in retrospect now, God didn't just begin there. At the Wednesday prayer, it was always kind of strange because this guy would always seem to end up in the same side of the room with me. I would always sit at the opposite end of where the main entrance door was. It would always seem like he would come over to my end of the room. I never quite understood why. I was upset with him over a situation and had never talked to him about it. Not too scriptural, but I had not done that. God had put him in my room. When I saw who it was, I laughed to myself. I said, "God, you surely have a sense of humor in this because I know what I'm going to have to do before the week's up." That was on Monday about noon. Monday was not a convenient day, Monday night, and then Tuesday, and Tuesday night. I kept thinking maybe we would be in the room together in the evening time after our session, but he stayed out later than I did. I was always asleep when he got there. Then I got up and out of the room before he was around. There wasn't a convenient time. Finally by Wednesday afternoon, the last session in the afternoon, I knew something had to be taken care of. I asked this gentlemen if he was busy after we finished our session. He said he didn't have anything going. I asked him if he could meet me in the room. When we were in the room together, I just asked him to forgive me because I had feelings in my heart that were not what God wanted. The hard thing on my part is I always want to be right. I wanted to explain why I had those feelings. God checked me on that and said,

"The reason is not important. What's important is that you harbored those feelings. That's what you need to deal with. The issue is a moot point at this level, at this time." One of the difficult things was for me to be able to not defend myself, to just simply ask for forgiveness. My roommate did something that was very important. He accepted my request for forgiveness without saying, "Oh, that's all right. It wasn't anything." Whenever you open your guts up to somebody, the last thing you need is for somebody to say, "Ah, don't think anything about it. It wasn't important." To graciously accept the repentance and grant it, I think are two very important things.

In summary, I think one of the greatest things God has done for me personally through the Prayer Summits is to draw me closer to people.

Q.   It seems the Lord is using the Prayer Summits to clean up areas in interpersonal relationships. Once those things are cleaned up He can use the Ministerium in much greater ways.

A.   Years ago I would never have admitted it. That's for me a very key thing. Just being alone, or together away from the local environment, from all the pressures and the phones and everything else, it gives time for that sort of thing to begin to take place. And again, the openness for it. If you are in a spiritual environment where you are willing to listen to the Lord, the

---

[Facing page.]

The 1999 Prayer Summit at Old Oak Ranch in Columbia. Eighty five Pastors gathered for the sixth summit and experienced the unmistakable presence of Christ.

Lord will tell you a lot of things. Not always what you want to hear, but He'll tell you a lot of things.

Q.   Why do you think God chose to begin such a work of unity in Modesto?

A.   I don't have the foggiest idea. The only thing I can tell you is it's just a sovereign move of God. I don't know why He would pick Modesto. I think probably we've all looked at a lot of reasons, but I don't have a good one. Except God in his sovereignty just began. I stumble around trying to explain it, but I don't know of any other reason. I mean, it wasn't because we were super good, it wasn't because we were super spiritual, and it certainly wasn't because we had been praying together. In fact going way back to that first Prayer Summit, one of the facilitators said something that kind of rubbed me the wrong way until I thought about it and prayed about it. He said, "You guys haven't been praying enough together. That's your big problem, you haven't been praying together." I thought who made you a judge over Israel? But the man was right, he was absolutely right. Even now five years into the equation, we're still at the very doorstep. It's not something we have arrived at or can say that we now pray enough together. We still are working at it.

Kevin Friesen said something after our first Community Praise Gathering. We had videotaped it and it was a great success. Requests were coming in [for copies]. Kevin said something to the Steering Committee. He said, and this is my paraphrase, "Gentlemen, we need to decide if we want to be in the business of seeking God, or if we want to be in the business of selling

tapes and telling people how to do it." I think uncon-
sciously, if not consciously, at that point we made a
determination that we wanted to be in the business of
seeking God and not in the business of selling tapes
and telling people how to do it. I just came back from
Light the Nations in Dallas. Don Christianson and I
both kind of cringed because they were using the term
"The Modesto Model." I almost kind of shuttered. Not
that it's wrong, but I'm not sure we've seen something
done here through human means. It's a God thing.
God is going to get the glory and He's not going to
share it with anybody, Modesto or Timbuktoo.

Q. What lessons or principles have you observed here in
Modesto which could help other communities bring
their churches together? While this fouls up your comment that we aren't necessarily in the business of mar-
keting something, but at the same tine we are being
observed by communities all across America. They
are asking, could the same thing happen in our community? If they're asking that question, do we have an
answer?

A. Last week I had the opportunity to be in a town on
the west edge of Houston, Texas. A little town by the
name of Katie. They have what they call the Church
of Katie there, which kind of grew out of an exposure
to the Church of Modesto. I went to pastors' prayer
there last Tuesday. They had twenty some people
in the room. A little small room which was wall-to-
wall people. They're doing similar things, though not
the same. In answer to this question, I think there
are principles people can understand and use, cross
culturally, inter city, however you want to think of it.
I think there are principles. I hesitate to say what

they are, lest people try to clone them. But I think there are a couple of them that are important. One of them is beginning to acknowledge we have a need. I don't think the churches in America really sense this as much as churches in other parts of the world. In the church in other parts of the world, there is a real need and they are locked into a real spiritual battle. We can't do the job alone. That is another lesson people have to come to understand. We can't do the job alone. I would like to see the day, and this isn't original with me, when we begin to identify what the giftings in the various churches are. We need to recognize that in the churches in the city one may be the berthing room, one may be the elementary school room, or one may be the emergency room where you take your basket cases. In the past I think we thought of our church, our local church, individually or denominationally, as having to be everything to all people. The fact is we aren't. I'm giving my opinion now. God is not located in any one church body in the community. If that were the case, we would be meeting in one super-huge building, and that's never going to happen. It won't happen because of differences in styles, personalities, etc. The number one lesson or principle, I think, is recognizing we have a need we can't meet ourselves. Let's reach out across the barriers we've erected over the years and let's tear those barriers down.

An interesting thing I've noticed is that if we become proud of what God has done and claim it for ourselves, God would walk away from it because He won't share His glory with anyone. We don't own this thing.

The principle of praying together is absolutely essential. You would never see what's happened in this city if we didn't pray together. I look at guys from charismatics to mainline denominational churches praying together. I never thought I'd see the day that one of my best friends was a Lutheran pastor. I recently said to another guy , "Before I met you, I didn't know anybody from the Reformed Church of America. I wasn't sure anything good could come out of it. God has taught me differently." I think the principle here is to respect one another. Along with that, we recently covenanted together that we would not speak evil of another brother or church. We focused, in the community as a whole, on who we are in Christ. Whether we come from the most somber or the most demonstrative worship service, our differences don't matter. What we speak of is who we are in Christ and how He's made us one.

C. OBSERVATIONS

1. The place to begin in developing unity is to acknowledge that we have needs, both for God and for His help in breaking down walls. Seeing the Prayer Summit as an essential time together did not come over night. Initially two of the multi-staff churches in town expected their staff to attend in order to facilitate involvement.

It is easy for the "tyranny of the urgent" to crowd out that which is truly important. Therefore, for a community of pastors to set this time aside and keep it a priority will take discipline and a commitment to the process. A ministerium must see this time of prayer as a nonnegotiable step towards unity. Programs will not create unity. Retreats will not create unity. Conferences, motivational speakers, and workshops will not create unity. Confession before the Lord, both individually and corporately, and seeking His face without an agenda or time line will serve to enhance unity as no other activity.

Second Chronicles 7:14: *If my people, who are called by my name, will humble themselves and pray and seek my face and turn from their wicked ways, then will I hear from heaven and will forgive their sin and will heal their land.*

2.   God is not willing to share His glory with any one. Once Modesto begins to take some recognition, God's blessing will be removed. The Prayer Summit is not about a church leading a program of prayer. It is not about a leader directing other leaders in prayer. It is about a group of servants on their knees seeking the one whom they serve. No church receives credit for "putting this retreat together." No pastor receives attention for "leading an effective time before the Lord." This is a time to seek God, confess before Him and listen to Him. It is a time for each pastor to be alone before their God and to come together as a group before their God. Whatever begins to happen in a community will not be a result of what the pastors have done, but what the Lord has chosen to do as a result of pastors humbling themselves before His sovereignty.

3. Praying together is absolutely essential if unity is to come. Praying together served to unite the Greater Modesto Ministerial Association in purpose, in its priorities and in its plan for unity and direction. The time together before the Lord solidified bonds of friendship, a sense that the pastors were on the "same team" rather than opposing parties. Worshipping together, singing together, praying together, taking communion together, and laughing together all enhanced the growing commitment to unity in the essentials accompanied with an acceptance of diversity in the nonessentials. Praying together unleashed God's supernatural powers available to a community of believers.

4. Using an outside organization, such as Northwest Renewal, provided a neutral facilitator which kept the atmosphere of the summit "safe" for all. This was not a "program" or conference put on by one church for the other churches. Other groups who have attempted to lead their own have had less success with their prayer summits.

5. Traveling outside the local area is a simple yet essential ingredient. It is imperative to limit distractions; the continual phone calls, parishioner needs, office pressures and deadlines, in order to enhance full involvement in a prayer summit. The money invested in "getting away" is well worth the return.

6. Many pastors have stated that the first or greatest step in their personal journey toward unity occurred on a prayer summit. Confessing, listening, worshipping, praying, communing, evaluating, uniting all occurred at these summits and served as the rallying point.

Chapter 5

WEDNESDAY PASTOR'S PRAYER MEETINGS

A. INTRODUCTION

At THE CONCLUSION OF the first Pastor's Prayer Summit in January, 1994, the pastors in attendance agreed that God would have them take another step to advance to a new level of unity for the community. The overwhelming consensus was that the pastors begin praying together on a weekly basis. Due to it's central location, First Baptist Church, was selected as the location. The first Wednesday following that first Prayer Summit began a weekly prayer meeting, which has now met regularly for over 240 weeks. Although the Minisiterium Chairman and usual prayer meeting facilitator is Pastor David Seifert, this interview is with Wade Estes, the Senior Pastor of First Baptist Church, which hosts the meeting. Pastor Wade is a man of great integrity, deep devotion to Christ and to his family, and also possesses a high level of commitment to prayer. Including the Wednesday Ministerium prayer hour, he and his pastoral staff pray together an hour each weekday morning, something very unusual for church staffs today.

B. INTERVIEW WITH PASTOR WADE ESTES [11]

Q. Pastor Wade, would you give a little background on yourself and how you are related to the Church of Modesto and specifically the Wednesday prayer time?

Wade Estes, Senior Pastor of First Baptist Church next to the building where Modesto's pastors have gathered for prayer each Wednesday since January of 1994.

Q. I was raised Roman Catholic and I was a faithful Catholic all the way through high school. My first year of college I decided there had to be more to God than trying to be good and sitting in church. I threw it all out and lived a pretty worldly lifestyle for about a year and a half. At the end of that year and a half I figured there had to be more to life than just partying. I was living in Mesa, Arizona at the time. The Lord started working in my life. I was involved in sports and ended up damaging one of my knees and having surgery. That kind of woke me up in terms of the direction in my life and what I really wanted from life. When my junior year at Arizona State began, I ran into some guys from Campus Crusade. They were passing out Bibles as I was registering, so I took one and started reading it. Some friends who went to a church in Mesa had asked me to play softball with them that summer. I went because I liked athletics, but I started getting exposed to the gospel and to people who really loved the Lord. They invited me to go to a college-age weekend retreat

It was about six months after that I met a man, named Jerry Collins, who was on the pastoral staff of that church, First Baptist [Church] of Mesa, Arizona. We started meeting together on a weekly basis in a men's group. I really began growing spiritually. About a year later after I felt called to the ministry. I finished up my bachelor's degree in journalism at Arizona State. By that time Jerry Collins had moved to Modesto to be on staff here [First Baptist Church]. He had trained here, gone to Mesa, and was returning to First Baptist [Church] of Modesto.

I was looking for a place for a ministry and to go to seminary. I looked at the various seminaries and most of them just had classroom work. I knew there was more to ministry than just classroom work. I wanted some practical training and this was the only place where I could get day-in and day-out training.

Sharon and I moved here in December, 1977, and applied for the intern program. We were accepted in March of that year. I started seminary. In January of 1980 I did a one-year residency, and at the end of the year I was asked to stay. I came on as the Minister of Evangelism, then took on the married twenties group. In 1987, Pastor Yeager went on a sabbatical for the summer and asked me if I'd be the Executive Pastor while he was gone. I guess the results were good because I kept that position. About two years after that I became the Associate Pastor, and in September of '91 became the Senior Pastor here. I've been functioning in that role since September, 1991.

Q.   Wade, please talk about the Wednesday prayer time and how First Baptist Church began hosting those.

A.   After our first Prayer Summit we were deciding what would be a point of action. At the conclusion of the first Prayer Summit, we were asking what should our action point be? Before the summit there were once a month ministerial meetings. We decided to sort of can that and meet every week for one hour, just to pray. Not a business time, but strictly a prayer time, to see what the Lord had for us. First Baptist was asked to host that time. We're downtown which made it easy for us, and made it easy for everybody else. We said sure and for the last five years we've been happy to host it every Wednesday, from noon to 1:00 pm.

Q.   How has the prayer time contributed to the sense of unity that exists here today?

A.   When you start praying with somebody it gets it off
     the human kind of agenda, even the human min-
     istry agenda. But when you're kneeling down next to
     somebody, praying with them and for them, and ask-
     ing them to pray for you, it's just a totally different dy-
     namic that starts happening. I think, too, that if you're
     going to pray genuinely, you've got to be right with
     the guys you're praying with. If you've been harboring
     anything, you've got to deal with it. If you've ever had
     words with somebody, you've got to deal with them if
     we're going to pray genuinely, not just going through
     an exercise. We saw this need for genuineness right
     from the first Prayer Summit. After that, guys were
     getting right with one another and dealing with either
     real or perceived issues which brought a spirit of har-
     mony and genuine prayer.

Q.   Who were the key people that played a part in the
     Wednesday prayer time?

A.   I believe it was what preceded the Wednesday prayer
     time was key. Just coming together for the first Prayer
     Summit. Dave Seifert called me and two other pas-
     tors in town, Steve Hanna at Trinity Presbyterian, and
     Damian Kyle at Calvary Chapel. He asked us if we'd
     get together for breakfast to talk with us about some-
     thing. At that breakfast, Dave rolled out this idea of
     getting together for a Prayer Summit. Because of what
     the Lord had already been doing in my life and in
     the life of this church, I just saw it as the next step
     of what He wanted to do. So I said sure, let's just
     find a time and go for it. The other fellows also were
     real open, but they had different kinds of governmen-
     tal structures in their churches and needed to go back
     and talk to some people. Then we met with the people
     from Northwest Renewal out of Portland.

It was a green light for the Prayer Summit. I've already mentioned that out of the Prayer Summit came the weekly prayer times. That was really the key in terms of leading the prayer times. Dave was the President of the Ministerial Association, so he was a natural to do it. I think this was a part of his dream all along, that we would really function as one church in Modesto and there could be harmony between all of us. He's done just an outstanding job of leading that time.

Q.   Had God done anything in your heart personally to prepare you for this movement of unity?

A.   The thing He did to prepare me and our staff in our church began in January, '92. I felt strongly lead that God wanted us to be a church of prayer. That was key to learning what it meant to abide in Christ. I started preaching on prayer in January of that year and culminated on Easter Sunday. I was preaching on prayer from the Gospels, Jesus' teaching on prayer and then Jesus' life of prayer. God just did something with that. He lit a fire in people's hearts. Our pastoral staff started meeting me for one lunch hour a week. Either pick Tuesday, Wednesday or Thursday, and we'd pray through the lunch hour. At first that just seemed like a huge thing to be willing to do. A whole hour a week. It just seemed like a huge commitment, but we did it. I was at each of the three and they would come to one.

After roughly six months, we took the next step and began praying on a daily basis, the first hour of each workday. Wednesday is the noon hour with the other pastors. That's our hour together!

We still do that. It sort of helped lay the groundwork so that when the Prayer Summit idea came along it was just like, "Okay, here it is, this is the next step." I think God had to do that in us and in my heart because if someone had come to me three years before and said, "Let's take a week with the other pastors in town to go away and pray," I would have said, "Don't you have enough to do? What in the world are you going to take a week and do something like that for?" I really think our staff prayer time was the essential preparation work so we could even be up to speed to say yes to such an idea.

Q. Were there any bench mark events or statistics with regards to the Wednesday prayer time that contributed to the Church in Modesto?

A. Of course coming out of that first Prayer Summit there were around forty guys who were showing up at the Wednesday prayer time. The next year it was up to about sixty, then it was like eighty, and now around 100. It's been an increasing type of involvement over the years in that way.

After each Prayer Summit we come back and say, "What would the Lord have us do? Do we keep doing this or do we not?" Each time we've chosen yes, this is what the Lord wants us to do. We've continued with it.

In terms of bench mark events, I think Promise Keepers [PK] was a big help. I think it was out of the pastors' Promise Keepers event in Atlanta that the seedling ideas of the Church of Modesto kind of began. Someone came up with calling it "Mo-Church."

Also, Promise Keepers had a major theme of breaking down denominational walls. It wasn't just the pastors doing something and praying together, but it was also the men in the churches. They went to these PK events and were hearing the same kind of things in terms of one in Christ, and breaking denominational and racial barriers. At the first Oakland conference there were a bunch of people from Modesto. Unbeknownst to us until we got there, we were bringing about 800 guys. Guys from First Baptist Church and their friends.

I ran into Bob Horner there. Bob had spoken here at First Baptist for a week of meetings. It ended up he was the MC at the conference in Oakland. He said, "I've heard that you guys have got 800 people coming to this conference. We've never had anybody bring that many before." I said, "I didn't know that. We just were encouraging people to go. It just kind of happened. We weren't shooting for any number or anything like that." He said, "Since I know you guys, do you care if I razz you through the week? It'll help me as the MC to have stuff to talk about." He started doing that and we got a lot of attention as a group. Frankly I was more concerned after it was over that it was going to be more of ahindrance anything like that." He said, "Since I know you guys, do you care if I razz you through the week? It'll help me as the MC to have stuff to talk about." He started doing that and we got a lot of attention as a group. Frankly I was more concerned after it was over that it was going to be more of a hindrance to the unity in Modesto than any kind of help because we were the ones who were pointed out. There were hundreds of other men from Modesto. We weren't the only ones there. I ended up having to lead the prayer time the very next Wednesday. We started by just sharing some of the neat stuff that the Lord did at the Promise Keepers events because so many of us had been there. I thought, this is going to be a real test for the reality of our unity.

The Spirit was so sweet and so good. Someone said something about how I handled myself there, because they interviewed me at one point, and [they] appreciated [me] not drawing attention to the congregation, but talking about the whole Church of Modesto. I said, "Boy, this really relieves me because I was afraid this might put a wedge between us." One of the guys said, "It would have, but they let all of us go to lunch early so then we forgave you." Everybody laughed. I thought, "Wow! This unity thing is really real! It's really real!"

The next year, 1996, when Oakland came around again, we all decided to register as being from the Church of Modesto [COM]. Let's not register from our individual churches. Let's all put down that we're from the Church of Modesto and go as a community, as the Church of Modesto. Someone came up with the COM tee-shirt idea that year as well.

Q. Would you share any supernatural experiences in which God demonstrated His handiwork in causing this movement? God putting his stamp of approval. What you just shared, the numbers and the people's response certainly is one of them, but let's talk about the prayer time.

A. We regularly have visitors from out of town. Guys have said I've heard of this, heard of what you guys were doing, and just wanted to come and see what was happening. There have been people come from out of the country as well. Some of them have heard about the Church of Modesto in their own country, which kind of blew all of us away.

One fellow from Africa said that he believed the Lord had told him that He was going to use what was happening here in Modesto to spread all over the world. I think even the fact that we're still doing it after five years is incredible. It's not like we don't have something else to do. It isn't like all of a sudden our schedules have slowed down. If anything, our schedules have become more intense. I think there has been more spiritual warfare. I know it's certainly been true in my life and in this church. Some of it is directly related to this.

One time a man named John, who works for the Modesto Gospel Mission, brought his wife who was having a health problem of some kind. I can't remember what it was but it was very severe. He asked if we would pray for her. We gathered around, laid our hands on her, anointed her with oil, and prayed for her. She experienced a supernatural healing. That was pretty incredible.

Q.   Why do you think God chose to begin such a work in Modesto?

A.   I don't have a clue. I really don't. I've thought of how in the New Testament the question's asked, "Can anything good come out of Galilee?" It wasn't like Galilee was the center of the universe or anything. Modesto is certainly not known as ..., if it's known for anything maybe it's Gallo Winery. I guess I would say, I really believe that Second Chronicles 7:14 is a universal pattern and promise. In other words,I know that it was given to Solomon for Israel, but as I look through scripture I see that whenever a people humble themselves and pray, that God hears them and He blesses them. I think God has chosen to honor David Seifert's desire to see unity among the churches. He worked on unity a long time without any apparent signs of fruitfulness. Then he basically challenged us, "will you pray?"

I guess I don't think it's a Modesto only kind of thing, or you have to be some sort of unique community where there's this special chemistry or something like that. I think it has to do with God honoring His promise.

Q.   What lessons or principles have you observed here in Modesto which could help other communities help bring their churches together?

A.   I think first that the vision gets birthed in somebody's heart. It may be one person. It may be a small group of two or three, but God lays it on them. It has to be a "God thing." It can't just be, "Oh, that community did it and it worked. Isn't that nice. Why don't we try it? Maybe neat things will happen here too." Rather than a genuine thing where we just want to respond to God and let Him do what He wants to do. Persevering and sticking with it no matter what. That becomes the test of the vision. If I really believe this is from God, I've got to hang with it. If it's not of God, then it's going to fizzle and go away. For instance, we're five years into this thing and we're still staying with it.

I think none of us knew we were going to end up being this unified as a result of prayer. But we just hung with the Ministerial Association, realizing it wasn't hitting the mark, and hoping that God would do something new. I've already mentioned Second Chronicles 7:14. God is going to honor His word. He doesn't promise to do that in any particular time frame. That's where perseverance comes in again. I think as we wait He sifts and tests our motives. Are we pursuing a flash in the pan thing or are we after a genuine work of God? If we are, that means we must hang in because He's the one who has to move. We can't manipulate Him! Those would be the key lessons I think I've observed.

C. OBSERVATIONS

1.   A key ingredient to Modesto's unity is perseverance. The Ministerium has met together for nearly five years of uninterrupted weekly prayer meetings. At it's inception, none of the Modesto Pastors wished for one more weekly meeting. Now most are highly committed to this prayer time. Success requires commitment. A group must make a long-term commitment to pray together to see the long-term benefits of praying together.

2.   An essential foundation to unity is a spirit of genuineness on the part of the members. This genuineness or authenticity can only be achieved through praying together. Walls do not immediately come down. Transparency is not achieved overnight. The willingness to be vulnerable takes time. But consistent prayer together promotes a safe arena for authenticity. Authenticity in turn promotes unity.

3.   Modesto's meeting location is centrally located, in the downtown area. For obvious reasons, this benefits all attenders. The potential danger is that the central church may become the focus or host. However, the intent remains to facilitate travel time for all involved. Having a consistent location also avoids the confusion of where the group meets on any given month. It is always at the same location.

4.   Christ is the central focus of the prayer time, not any single leader. Though good leadership is crucial, this is not a business meeting; prayer and worship are the purpose for meeting. As such, there is no agenda or program for the time together. It is Spirit-led rather than pre- orchestrated.

5.   Worshipping is an integral part of the weekly time together before the Lord. Learning to sing together facilitates unity. There is no song leader. There are no song sheets, overhead transparencies or multi- media projections. Eyes are closed. Heads are bowed. Any pastor is free to lead out in accappella song as the Spirit moves his heart. The emphasis on the "tools" of singing are removed and men are free to worship from the heart.

Chapter 6

PRAY GREATER MODESTO

A. INTRODUCTION

IT WAS the summer of 1997. The Modesto Ministerium was faced with the decision of whether to hold a crusade in 1998. If so, which organization should be called upon. For several years they had sensed it was not yet time to move in that direction, but that God was still working on the unity issue as a foundation for evangelism. In 1997 one proposal came before them, only to be rejected. Shortly after that decision to wait for a green light from the Lord, the leadership was contacted by Ed Silvoso. While ministering in Argentina he had been impressed to contact Modesto about leading a Prayer Evangelism Crusade there. He did contact them. His proposal was considered and prayed about. In the fall of 97 the Church of Modesto embarked on a path which, to quote Robert, "has made all the difference." The PRAY GREATER MODESTO crusade was held over two weeks in February of 1998. Unlike other crusades whose fruit is questionable six months later, Modesto is a different place since the Prayer Evangelism Crusade. The ripples are still being felt all over the city.

Ed Silvoso introduced four phases of the Lighthouses of Prayer Ministry through the Crusade:

PHASE I   Establish a Perimeter of Faith (Luke 10:5)

PHASE II   Build Bridges (Luke 10:7)

PHASE III   Pray for "Felt Needs" (Luke 10:9)
PHASE IV   Proclaim the Kingdom (Luke 10:9)

The Pray Greater Modesto Crusade has now been transformed into what is called Lighthouses of Prayer. The emphasis is on establishing a "Lighthouse of Prayer" in a home within each neighborhood of Modesto.

God has used Ed Silvoso for years in crusade outreaches with his brother-in-law, evangelist Luis Palau. Ed founded Harvest Evangelism to assist the Church in Argentina. Ed and his team have developed a Biblical plan to reach entire cities for Christ through prayer evangelism. This prototype has been successful in his home country of Argentina, It is now proving itself effective in the U.S. as well.

B. INTERVIEW WITH ED SILVOSO, [12]
OF HARVEST EVANGELISM

Q.   Ed, how did you happen to become involved with the Church of Modesto?

A.   I knew about the Church of Modesto and the unity through the Promise Keepers's publications. I knew God was doing something there. We also heard about the Heaven's Gates and Hell's Flames play and the incredible number of decisions there. I was in Argentina in July, '97. We were experimenting with a new principle, the one of how to change the climate of a city. We saw extra-ordinary results. While I was praying about it, I felt the Lord impressing on my heart, "Call the pastors in Modesto because they have the unity that is such a prerequisite for this to happen." When I came back I called Wade Estes and David Seifert and told them about it. I then went and met with them. The rest is history.

Q. How do you think the prayer movement has contributed to the great sense of unity here in Modesto?

A. I would say the fact that the pastors dare take outside of the prayer room what they were doing there, and challenge first their leaders and then their members to do the same thing. The climax of that, at least the first climax, (there are many more that we haven't reached yet,) was that prayer walking. When a member from one church bumps into a member of another church, I think that solidified in the hearts of the few people that we are one church indeed. It's not just that the pastors pray together, but we are one church.

The other factor, I believe, is the radio programs that were done Monday through Wednesday. Because of those radio programs, we heard so many members say, "We felt pastored." We took it to mean, "We felt that our pastors were ministering to us, the church." In a sense, Modesto became a living parable of what is a city-wide church.

Q. Ed, Why do you think God has been moving in the hearts of Modesto's Churches and Christians?

A. It's a mystery, you know, known only to God. But, I believe perhaps a seed that Billy Graham left fifty years ago has to do with it. I would say that's one factor.

The other one is, and again only God knows the true story, but you have some unique features here. You have charismatics and non-charismatics working together. Then you have high caliber leadership. I'm amazed at how time and again God uses Dave Seifert.

He's a humble guy, but he has his eye on the ball and he doesn't go for it. He points to the ball until everybody sees it and then he says "Charge." I would say that's another factor. You have good leadership in place.

Q.   What were some lessons, principles, that you would offer? I know they're in the book, but can you share maybe three or four lessons that are transferable to other communities?

A.   What Modesto proved in America is that you can change the climate of a city. You can change it. The fact that they did a Sunday morning city-wide church service telecast, that was new ground. Unknown to me. Now, the videotape that came out of that has made the rounds. That videotape has been seen around the world. Out of that came hope for America. Now New York, Houston, big cities are going for it here. I would say the greatest contribution of Modesto was to produce a prototype that Americans can embrace. It made the Argentine event principles transcultural.

Q.   So you can change the climate in a city, and secondly, to show the rest of America specifically how and where it can be done.

A.   Yes, especially the how. Two other things that are now becoming a standard are the youth emphasis and the ethnic participation and partnership. You can have three levels: participation, partnership and leadership. Here in Modesto you had ethnic involvement in partnership and leadership. That has cast the DNA, so to speak, for the other cities as well.

Those three levels of involvement are: participation, where people just come; partnership, where they do it together; and leadership, "let me lead." In Modesto you have moved the ethnic dimension above the participation to partnership and leadership. That model is being copied all over America.

Q. Ed, most people are aware that there has been some criticism of your ministry. Maybe this would be a good opportunity for you to respond to some criticism. If I might simplify one of the criticisms, it might be that lines between the charismatics and the non-charismatics are being blurred?

A. I think, in the scriptures we see a continuing. Where evil increases, but so the outpouring of the Holy Spirit increases. The prayer of Jesus is that we become one. We're not getting farther from it, but closer to it. I believe we will keep up the same thing, but we will emphasize our common factors. I'm not threatened by that because I do counselling to pastors, and it doesn't make any difference whether they speak in tongues or not. The human heart is the human heart. But there are prophets of doom, fear and anger. There are people who thrive on those negative emotions, but they are losers. The sunset is already over the horizon. This is unstoppable, I mean it's happening all over America. Who can stop that?

Q. This is a movement of the Holy Spirit that is occurring throughout America and throughout the world?

A. Yes, and that's why I don't take any credit for it. Because God is doing it

Q. Can you share a story from Modesto that would be your favorite, maybe, of how you saw God working in an instance?

A.   Don Gerlach's story is a remarkable one. He tells it this way:

On Monday evening, February 23, Linda, my second wife, and I were following the "Lighthouses of Prayer" radio broadcast on KCIV radio. While we were listening to the broadcast, my adopted son, Patrick called and wanted to borrow some money. I hadn't seen him in twelve years.

On Tuesday evening I was alone and again listening to the KCIV broadcast when surprisingly, Patrick again showed up unannounced. I invited him in to listen to the broadcast with me. He said he had been listening to KCIV Radio regularly and was aware of these special events. As we sat there, Ed Silvoso was speaking about families coming together and reconciliation happening. That seemed to move him to personalize his own situation. Patrick started to talk about his previous 11 years since I had been taken away from his life. He detailed a very sordid lifestyle during that time which I knew nothing about.

I told him, "Patrick, God can forgive all this mess. He is bigger than all that you have done." As the broadcast ended, we were invited to continue to reflect on the things we had just heard. I knew if there was to be any reconciliation, I had to ask for his forgiveness So I said, "Because of my sin, a divorce occurred. Patrick, would you please forgive me for the divorce which played a major part in your lifestyle of sin?" He said yes and asked if I would forgive him as well. What he confessed really tore at me and opened some deep emotional pain. In tears I said, "Yes." Patrick was also crying and very contrite over the event.

In the middle of all that emotion, he said something I'll never forget, "Don, will you be my dad again?" An avalanche of tears rooted in the deep emotional pain began to flow. They were cleansing, healing and reconciliatory, far beyond anything I could have dreamed of. We held each other for some time and I knew I had two sons again. Later he said he had felt responsible for the divorce. I assured him that he was not, and had it not been for my own sins, the family would have stayed together. The burden he had been carrying all those years was lifted. Patrick had a dad again.

Now in August, 1998, Patrick is attending Calvary Chapel and is faithfully walking with the Lord.

My younger son, Brian, came to the Lord six days later. I believe it is due to the general spiritual atmosphere change brought about in this city during the radio broadcasts. All I can say is, "Thank you, Lord!"

Isn't that a tremendous story? If I had to recognize one thing in Modesto, it would be the 278 Wednesdays that the pastors have prayed, non- stop, at the pastors' prayer meetings. That's the backbone. Now the challenge that Modesto faces is to go to the next level and really, really take the church to the city. They are doing it, but they haven't done it totally yet. That's the next challenge. When you do that, you begin to see thousands of conversions every week. I see it in Latin America. Why not Modesto?

C.   INTERVIEW WITH TODD HUNNICUTT [13]

Todd Hunnicutt is the Coordinator for Lighthouses of Prayer for the Church of Modesto. His perspective and information bring a solid overview of the Pray Greater Modesto Crusade, and presents us with a picture of what is currently happening in Modesto. Todd, and his wife Sarah, are Mission candidates at First Baptist Church, and hope to be serving as missionaries in an international setting in the near future.

Q.   Introduce yourself and please give a little of your background and how you are related to the Church of Modesto.

A.   I'm Todd Hunnicutt, a missionary intern at First Baptist Church of Modesto. I am presently serving the Church of Modesto as Coordinator of the Lighthouses of Prayer to creatively encourage the believers of Modesto to reach their circle of influence by prayer, loving service and witness.

I have grown up attending First Baptist Church and have been involved in virtually every department in the church. I have also been a first-hand observer of the changes which have taken place due to the Church of Modesto movement.

In the fall of 1997, Ed Silvoso came to Modesto and began a movement that continues today. He helped launch Pray Greater Modesto (PGM), a citywide effort by many of the churches of Modesto to win our city for Christ. The PGM effort was certainly only possible after many years of prayer and cooperation between these churches. The first major coordinated effort was the Flood Relief, and PGM was the first time we as a church were stepping out to directly expand the kingdom of God and fulfill the Great Commission together. As we head into the next fall, we are seeing a tendency of some to look back on PGM, rather than see this as something ongoing. It should be more than "something ongoing," and literally be the focus of our churches and our coordinated efforts until Christ comes back!

Individual believers and families were asked to become Lighthouses of Prayer to their circles of influence. We decided to change the name from PGM to Lighthouses of Prayer to show this is an ongoing ministry of believers, whether or not they live in the greater Modesto area and to give it a title less event focused. My job today is to keep the ball rolling through creative means, basically to get tools into the hands of pastors and coordinate efforts. The churches are free to be involved at any level they choose or to develop their own promotional means.

Q. How did your ministry contribute to the great sense of unity that the Church of Modesto is experiencing today?

A. I find myself in a unique position, since nothing has ever been done over a long period of time between the Churches of Modesto except prayer between the pastors. There have been the two citywide rallies, the flood relief, the National Day of Prayer and many other events, but no ongoing coordinated effort. My task is something all the pastors want to have done and don't have time to do themselves. They always are very appreciative of the "kick in the pants" I give.

That "kick" is really their desire for the lost to be reached. I really believe this is the greatest aspect of unity in Modesto and the thing that will affect change in the greatest way on how each church functions, what their programs are and generally how they "do church." In the long run, we will probably need to change the way things are done to make our churches more friendly to the pre-Christian, and to facilitate believers reaching out instead of building our own kingdoms.

I believe this will also serve to expand the circle of unity in Modesto. Some might see a weekly prayer meeting as a waste of time or of little value. Many pastors on the Westside of Modesto must work second jobs. They cannot join us for the prayer time, but they could join us through prayer the rest of the week. By God's grace, as we step out and actually see large numbers of Modestans coming to Christ, others will want to join in. As citywide evangelistic efforts are built on the foundation of prayer, others will see the need to join.

I see Lighthouses of Prayer (LP) as the reason for our unity, and non-believers will see us working together to serve and preach the gospel in our community. The fulfillment of the Great Commission has too often been put off by lesser concerns. It has certainly been hampered by our fighting, or worse, our indifference among ourselves. LP has been widely accepted in Modesto by believers who have previously been afraid to share their faith (myself included) as a means of reaching people by relying more on God's power through prayer than their powers of persuasion. If we can keep the momentum going, the believers of Modesto will win their own city.

Q.   Who were the key people who played a part in your ministry?

A.   The Steering Committee of the Greater Modesto Ministerial Association is the primary group that got PGM and LP going. They chose the less public, more grassroots Prayer Evangelism mode over the stadium crusade model by inviting Ed Silvoso to come to Modesto. David Seifert's leadership of the GMMA

Ed Silvoso is a visionary who can relate across lines of conservative/evangelical/charismatic division. Before he came we viewed evangelism in a different light, and his influence as an "outsider" and as an expert in his field, I believe, helped to convince many of the value of Prayer Evangelism as a viable model for ministry and not merely an alternative for evangelism whimps.

Don Christiansen, the first coordinator, had gone to Argentina to see this same process begun in the city of San Nicholas. He came back to serve as the Co-ordinator for PGM. The Lord had moved him, rather strangely, out of a successful pastorate, but when PGM came along it was clear what the Lord was doing. Don implemented the ideas of Silvoso and the Steering Committee in an incredible way, pulling off some things no one had ever done before. But by the summer of 98' it became clear that God was moving Don into church planting and an increased role as chaplain of the local Hospice. That was when he turned to me, having served on his "Action Team" of lay people. At his suggestion, the Steering Committee hired me as a consultant to the Church of Modesto to keep LP going.

Jeff Kreiser is another key player, who was able to take some of the more advanced issues of web site, television broadcast and promotional video and make them reality. Having used many of these same tools in his church plant, he was a great resource for Don in PGM, and continues to serve in a variety of capacities.

Q.   Had God done anything in your heart to prepare you personally for this movement of unity?

A.   I had always struggled with the division between believers, but I did nothing to stop it. Being from a large church it was not very necessary to work with other Christians. Something between resentment and jealousy would characterize some of my attitudes. Then in my college years, various friends would become dissatisfied with First Baptist Church and look elsewhere. My resentment grew toward churches they went to. Also the best known ecumenical movements involved mainline denominations and liberal churches, and even the term "ecumenical" smacked of heresy and a non-productive unity.

As many of the pastors started praying together it did seem like a good idea, and the news we heard coming out of those meetings was good. When our missions pastor left for the mission field, I was brought on as the Interim Director of Missions for our church. I started attending the prayer meetings on Wednesdays. It was a very powerful time. Though I didn't mix much, I saw the value in it.

When my wife, Sarah, and I went to Albania for a six month exploratory trip in mission, we went with a great love of the diversity in the Church of Modesto and a desire to see it spread. I had recently read Primary Purpose by Ted Haggard and was excited about the possibilities. In Albania there was great cooperation among the group of missionaries we were with, but there were clear divisions between the non-orthodox Church Christians. In that city of 70,000, the five or so churches were very divided and suspicious of each other. We weren't able to affect much change in that area and we were very dissatisfied with the situation there at that time.

When we returned to the U.S., I did not return to the Wednesday prayer time as I didn't feel I had a place there without an official ministry position. But as a custodian at church I would set up for the prayer time, and I'd read what was passed out in cleaning up after. In January of 1998, I felt the Lord telling me very clearly to return to the Wednesday prayer time, so I took the time off each week and even got to go on the Prayer Summit. I really felt that this was where I needed to be every week. Six months later I got this position, which was far greater than I could have ever imagined. I have come full circle from a suspicion of unity efforts, to a strong desire to make this a part of my ministry wherever God calls us.

Q. Were there any bench mark events or statistics with the Lighthouses of Prayer which contributed to the great sense of unity?

A. The key events have largely been described above, but I'll examine them a little closer. Sometime in mid-1997 initial meetings were held between Ed Silvoso and the Steering Committee of the GMMA. October 1997 was the first meeting with Silvoso and the whole group of pastors in GMMA; there was a great turnout that day. In January 1998 was the large training time, held at First Baptist Church, where Ed led hundreds of leaders from various churches in becoming Lighthouses of Prayer. There was another training time the final Saturday before the first simulcast. That day also offered specialized training to business people and intercessors. The youth had a huge training with 860 students involved. Their training was less theoretical involving going out to the campuses that same day.

The Sunday simulcast was a landmark day and very exciting, a broadcast led by Silvoso from the "Pastor's Prayer Room." Most of the broadcast was Silvoso talking and leading the people in interactive prayer. The next three evenings were hour-long radio broadcasts led by Silvoso and several area pastors. Monday night was a time of dedication of homes to be Lighthouses, including anointing the doors of our homes with oil and signing a Certificate of Dedication. Many people said they first saw who are their other Christian neighbors that night as they stepped out to anoint their doors. Tuesday night was cleansing night, where people were urged to physically or symbolically put a wastebasket in the living room and put anything in it that shouldn't be in the home. Wednesday night was the prayer walk, where Silvoso and the pastors led as people walked their neighborhoods. The broadcast wasn't particularly suited to the prayer walking, and many just turned off the radios and prayed. Many encounters that night happened between believing neighbors. That week was also a city-reachers school hosted by Silvoso, and the churches got to work together to host the people that came.

A month later there was another TV simulcast, but this time the format was largely testimonies and was again hosted by Silvoso. Another very powerful time as we heard what God was doing in our town. Again the sense that believers all over the city were gathering, watching this and praying together was very exciting. That week, which was Palm Sunday week, we only had two radio broadcasts. Instead of a radio broadcast-led prayer walk, people were urged to stand up, go out and pray after the broadcast ended. A Spanish broadcast also began.

In May the ongoing local Christian TV program on the TV station that had done the simulcasts, "The Eleventh Hour," volunteered to begin focusing on Lighthouses every week for an hour. A gift was given to sponsor a half hour radio broadcast every Saturday night on the same radio station that had led in the prayer focus weeks. We still have no idea of how many folks are listening and watching, but they've been good tools to keep it fresh.

Fall 1998 was a new phase in Lighthouses, with tools developed to enable churches to do it themselves. The theme was Lighthouses to the marketplace, emphasizing the third stage of prayer evangelism, which is praying for peoples felt needs. Instead of another simulcast, we developed a sixteen minute video which could be used in each church whenever they desired. It celebrates the 50th anniversary of Billy Graham's early crusade in Modesto and the new direction of prayer evangelism today. The new tool that was introduced in the video is the "How Can I Pray For You?" plastic card which can be made into a button, hung from a purse or bag, or placed near a persons workstation to encourage the believer toward greater awareness and holiness, and to request prayer requests from people around us.

Q. Would you share any supernatural experiences in which God demonstrated his handiwork in causing this movement?

A. Pray Greater Modesto was filled with amazing things and testimonies. In the second simulcast we heard several testimonies. Probably the most remarkable was the testimony of a pastor's son. He had fallen away into borderline occult activity and had a vision of Christ sitting next to him in a restaurant, and his conversion that followed.

A local college girl overheard a conversation in a restaurant where two people were amazed about the changes in Modesto. They couldn't put their finger on it, but they knew something had changed.

Q. Why do you think God chose to begin such a work of unity in Modesto?

A. I have no idea. God's sovereignty is a fascinating topic for me. Like his choice of me to be His adopted child, there was nothing in Modesto to recommend us to Him. Certainly there is a great heritage here. The co-operation among the pastors has been great. But to think that Modesto is now a model being proclaimed all over the world is truly baffling, humbling and exciting.

Q. Do you see any down side to this movement of Unity?

A. I believe Christ's commands and prayers for unity among believers are among the most neglected verses of the Bible. The move from monthly ministerial meetings and luncheons, to weekly prayer, to working together in flood relief, to Lighthouses of Prayer was the greatest thing that could have happened. A local pastor, who recently accepted a call elsewhere, said the thing that hurt even greater than leaving the church he had pastored was leaving the unity of pastors in Modesto.

One negative thing that came out of our Pray Greater Modesto Crusade occurred the first night of the radio broadcast, when a local pastor's wife spoke on the broadcast. Some conservatives felt she was preaching or teaching or doing something the Bible prohibited women to do. Some just didn't like her style. Regardless of who was right, it was interesting that here in the first moments of the Church of Modesto stepping out in faith to reach our community, Satan used this to divide. Some very vocal people left churches over it. One man told his pastor, who was in the studio as part of the broadcast, that he should have gotten up and walked out in protest. Thankfully he didn't! This was a bench mark event in that it didn't destroy the movement either by those who supported his being there being disgusted at the narrow-mindedness of the others, or by those who found her presence there unbiblical, regarding the COM as heretical.

Even with that, I see absolutely no negative sides to the Church of Modesto. There are problems, and there will certainly be misunderstandings, accusations, etc. But we cannot ignore Christ's admonition toward unity any longer. Those who place a higher value on lesser issues will only hurt the Body of Christ by their inaction. We must go forward and pray blessings on pastors who have not yet joined the movement that God might draw them in.

Q. What lessons or principles have you observed here in Modesto which could help other communities bring their churches together?

A. Like the pastor who is leaving, I never want to work in a place where the churches are fighting. As one headed into missions, I am probably setting myself up for disappointment, since conflict between missionaries is the key reason for missionaries returning home. But I will do everything in my power as I move overseas to enter with a servant's attitude of helping facilitate unity among the believers.

First you must be convinced of the biblical necessity of "brothers dwelling together in unity." It cannot merely be something that would be nice to do. It must be a burning desire. Something you build into your schedule to accomplish, as much as you place priority on preparing to preach each Sunday. You must pastor your city, and you cannot do it alone. You must begin a movement in personal prayer, seeking God's face as to how to proceed. In Modesto, the Pastors Prayer Summits really sparked it. Extended times of prayer are key. Maybe you could then move on to pray with a few other pastors who you know would be receptive to the idea.

Focus on Christ, and the unity will come. Focus on unity, and Christ may not ever be allowed to come! Let prayer time together be the foundation. Unstructured, honest prayer. Don't take a package deal from elsewhere and try to cram your city into it. Except for the Prayer Summit, which itself really has no structure, we have always taken things and adapted it to our city. There is no formula. Even my suggestions are merely that.

Each pastor must take it upon themselves individually to widen the circle of prayer, by praying for loving pastors outside the circle. This is something we aren't very focused on yet. If this is to continue, we must reach out or the lines will become more defined and the walls higher, of those in the Church of Modesto and those outside.

You "gotta" keep going. Yes we've had some remarkable advances and amazing things happen, but the Great Commission is not accomplished in Modesto, much less the rest of the world. You must plan for the long haul and not give up if everything doesn't turn out as you want right away. Things may never be as you want them, but if you are seeking God together, they will be as He wants them.

Decisions should rest with a Steering Committee or some small body picked from within the larger prayer context. If everyone is in on all the discussion, too many voices will make for gridlock and not everyone will be able to be really educated on all matters. Decisions, not prayer, will become the focus. In that group there should be a good representation of big and small churches, ethnic groups, old church and church plants, old-time residents, and new folks.

Never underestimate the power of symbols. Our simple Church of Modesto tee-shirts became a true unifying force: (1) as I buy and wear it I am reminded of my unity with other believers, and (2) as I see others wearing it I am encouraged by seeing them or by going up and speaking with them. The Church of Modesto logo is now a recognized thing around town. The placards with the Lighthouse on them are incredible. People are seeing them all over and pondering the connection. Nonbelievers are asking about them. We are seeing Jehovah's Witnesses avoiding homes with Lighthouses. The upcoming Got Needs? Campaign will introduce another key symbol that will hopefully be recognized citywide; we may even introduce it with media ads to heighten visibility.

You have to do it. To be a follower of Christ and not seek fellowship, camaraderie and the power of working together with other believers is wrong. You must pay the price and be obedient to the clear commands of Scripture and do it, today!

D. OBSERVATIONS

1. The starting point for unity is a deep conviction of the Biblical mandate for unity. Who God gives that vision to initially is not as important as the need that the ministers of a community rally behind it. It could be a lay person who starts calling a community to unity. For a community to reach the level of unity Modesto has, it is essential that the pastors take the lead in it.

2. Each pastor must assume responsibility to pray for his personal sphere of influence,which must include names of other pastors to join in. For lay people to embrace the vision and practice of unity, they must witness their pastors modeling it first. In Modesto that has clearly taken place, as this study attests to.

3. Never underestimate the power of symbols in communication and ministry, such as the Church of Modesto logo (COM) on tee-shirts, placards etc. These serve the purpose of reminding the people of what God is doing in our community as well as providing the opportunities to communicate with others both the Gospel as well as the vision for church unity.

4. Praying a blessing on people, Christian or not, represents the heart of God. Each person in the COM, pastors and lay people, have been encouraged to pray blessings on the people within their sphere of influence. These two words, praying and blessing, represent the heart of God. He wants to hear from Christians and He wants to bless people.

5.   We should not speak with a person about God until we have spoken to God about that person. This is the essence of Prayer Evangelism. This is what gives evangelism it's power. "Prayer is the most tangible trace of eternity in the human heart. Intercessory prayer on behalf of the felt needs of the lost is the best way to open their eyes to the light of the gospel." [14]

6.   It was the goal of the COM to have a Lighthouse of Prayer in each neighborhood in Modesto. Emphasis was placed upon their membership in the COM more than in their local church. In two of the Modesto churches, a map of home churches is posted with other churches home churches charted together with their own. They have enlarged thier vision to see the city from God's perspective, not just their own.

7.   "Cities are central to God's redemptive strategy. The Great Commission begins with a city, Jerusalem ... In order to fulfill The Great Commission, we must reach every city on earth with the Gospel." [15]

SECTION THREE

PARACHURCH
IN A SUPPORTING ROLE

"Christianity is the total plan for the human machine. We have all departed from that total plan in different ways, and each of us wants to make out that his own modification of the original plan is the plan itself. You find this again and again about anything that is really Christian: every one is attracted by bits of it and wants to pick out those bits and leave the rest. That is why we do not get much further: and that is why people who are fighting for quite opposite things can both say they are fighting for Christianity."[16]

C.S. Lewis

In addition to experiencing harmony within it's churches Modesto has had the unusual blessing of benefitting from a similar cooperative effort from the ranks of the parachurch organizations. Four such ministries are CLEAN (a political action organization); The Modesto Union Gospel Mission; Promise Keepers, and Youth For Christ. Each of these groups has provided a place where Christians from all of Modesto's churches can serve along side one another and both cultivate unity as well as reap it's rewards.

Included in this section are interviews with three of these ministry leaders. An interview with Rick Fritzmeyer, director of Stanislaus YFC and leader in the Youth Pastors Network, is found in chapter fourteen.

Chapter 7

CLEAN

(Citizens Leading Effective Action Now)

A. INTRODUCTION

CLEAN *(Citizens Leading Effective Action Now)* is a grass-roots political action organization which is non-profit and non-sectarian. It seeks to communicate the righteousness of God in the forefront of the political community, and by upholding the morality laid down in the Commandments of God.

CLEAN,the largest organization of it's kind in the western United States, boasts a membership of 4,350. That is due largely to the involvement of the Church of Modesto. Harry Kullijian, CLEAN's president, is a man of intense conviction, great vision and high energy. He possess a wealth of information about the political process both in Modesto and statewide. Harry has been an active member of First Baptist Church for nearly thirty years. Nearly eighty, this amazing man continues to operate a business, fly his private airplane and lead the CLEAN organization.

B. INTERVIEW WITH HARRY KULLIJIAN [17]

Q. Harry, would you please give a little of your background and CLEAN's background? Also tell how you are related to the Church of Modesto.

A.   First of all, my name is Harry Kullijian. I am seventy nine years old. I've been involved in this work [CLEAN] for almost twenty one years.

I was born of Armenian parents. When they migrated to America, fleeing the genocide of the Armenian nation just prior to and during World War I, they were leaving primarily because of religious persecution. My background has been one of great gratitude that I live in America. I've always tried to be, as a young man, cognizant of community service. From that my life began to progress.

I became a member of the Modesto City Council in 1972. It was just following the near bankruptcy of my financial resources. I sought the Lord for two years. I was fifty years old then, asking the Lord to heal me, to touch my life and to provide for me what service I may give.

Q.   Would you tell us when and how you came to Christ?

A.   After serving in World War II, I served in China, Burmese, and the India Theater. I was married in 1942 in San Bernardino, California. When I returned home a friend of mine, Dr. Al Barrian, who is still a very dear brother of mine, took us to a Christian Businessmen's Association National Convention in the St. Frances Hotel in San Francisco in September, 1947. Some of the great men of the nation were there giving their testimonies. One of them happened to be R.J. LaTourneau, the famous Christian businessman and founder of LeTourneau College in Longview, Texas. The comment he made was, "No matter how much I give to the Lord, He out gives me every time. I give it to Him by the thimble full, and He gives it back." Gerry and I said, "We need to stand up and make a decision for the Lord, Jesus Christ". We did, and that was in 1947, and my life has been changed so dramatically since then.

We adopted two children. I was recalled into the service during the Korean War. When I came back I moved to Turlock in 1951. I started a construction business. In the meantime we were really looking for a church. Ultimately we have spent twenty five years at First Baptist Church.

In 1972 I ran and became a member of the City Council. It was at that time I think the Lord was actually preparing me for the ultimate work that I was to do. As a councilman I learned a lot about what you do in politics, and yet at the same time I was in training for what I was eventually to do. I went to the City Council and tried to get them to pass ordinances. For example, prohibit pornographic magazines being close to residential areas or schools. I failed miserably.

One night as I came home late from a council meeting, my wife was watching television. There were three pastors on television. One was a Jew, one a Catholic, and one was Bill McNurney from Los Angeles. They were talking about two motion pictures being produced in Europe. One was called Many Faces of Jesus which portrayed Jesus as a homosexual. Incidently, there's another picture being made in the in the United States that does the same thing. The second one was The Passover Plot, which was Jesus Christ taking drugs to fake his death on the cross. My emotions, as I sat in the chair and I listened to this television program, I don't know what happened. I honestly believe the Lord touched my heart. It was blasphemy in the worst sense. I wrote a letter to the largest distributer and owner of motion picture theaters in California, named George Mann. I said, "Please don't show these films. Don't distribute these films should they come to California."

At the next Council meeting I said, "Jesus Christ is the center of my life. This is blasphemy. I would be absolutely wrong, it would be terribly wrong, for me to sit in this Council meeting and not say to you that I would encourage a ban on these movies by an ordinance passed by the City Council if they should come to the United States." That raised a national furor because of freedom of speech and so forth. But I didn't realize it at the time. I really had the power as a government official. Government can actually censor. It's private citizens that don't have the right of censorship. I got bombarded.

Eventually I found an organization in New York City run by a Jesuit Priest, named Father Hill. I talked to him several times and he was so impressed he came out to California and said, "I'm going to make you State Chairman of the State of California Morality in Media." Morality in Media went on for about three years.

There was so little interest in what was going on that I just forgot about the pornography situation. Then a group got together here in Modesto, which included Ross Kelly, Bud LaCore, and Doris Reis. They petitioned the City of Modesto to pass an ordinance regulating adult bookstores. The City Council of Modesto said they would do that. The group came to me and asked if I would get involved with this group. Bud LaCore was the main fellow. They asked me to be

President. I went before the Ministerium in 1983. Pastor Seifert was head of the Modesto Ministerium. I said, "If you are willing to support the efforts of CLEAN in the City of Modesto, I will accept the presidency of the organization. If you are not interested in supporting the efforts of CLEAN, then I am not going to waste my time because it cannot be done without the church." Pastor Seifert asked everybody to join hands around the tables as they prayed. The answer was yes, they would support. From that point on we began to have weekly meetings of CLEAN and the organization began to grow.

Q.   How did your ministry contribute to the great sense of unity to the Church of Modesto?

A.   I visited Don Stahl, the District Attorney. We had a core group of women who went all over town to talk — to the library, the police chief, to various groups, to stores and so forth, and come back with a report. We knew the Lord had said, "To prepare to battle, you've got to know who your enemy is and count your resources." We made a large folder of what existed in our community. We weren't guessing, we knew because we spent the first year doing nothing else but educating ourselves.

When I went to see the District Attorney Don Stahl, I told him what CLEAN was all about and that we were here to help. We wanted to do what we could do in the community to make a better place for all of us. As I was getting up to leave he said, "You haven't asked me to do anything." He was surprised because usually public officials are asked to do something or criticized for not doing something. I said, "Don, the Holy Spirit will either move you to do it, or He won't. If you don't do it, God will only give me another opportunity and another alternative." That changed his life to the point I was able to witness to the District Attorney. From that day on we have luncheon meetings every month. We have done it now for the last twelve years. We just revel in what the Lord is doing in our lives and how wonderful He is. We've become the closest of friends.

Q.   How did CLEAN contribute to the sense of unity in Modesto?

A.   It was the fact that it drew people together behind a common cause. When the people of God respond to the call of God, whatever that might be, a power unimaginable is released! The churches were allowing CLEAN, supporting CLEAN, and by their support and acknowledgement of CLEAN, they gave CLEAN the sustenance to magnify the glory of Christ in the community. That's the way I would put it.

At least 80% of our efforts in the area of pornography was to inform and to educate. We wanted to tell the community that pornography is related to teenage pregnancy, child abuse and rape. We have one of the highest rates here in Stanislaus County. I went to the churches and they printed it in the paper. When the churches united behind it, it was a marvelous thing to see.

Q.   Who were the key workers in CLEAN?

A.   Bud LaCore was a mentor, a brother in Christ, and the key player on the Board of Directors. Pastor Yaeger was my Pastor, always there to support the effort of CLEAN. Pastor Seifert was supportive of CLEAN. Joe Wright, Pastor of Calvary Temple was behind it.

Mary Davis is on the Board of Directors. Mary is a key person in CLEAN. Her organization, Letter Writers Make a Difference, has 250 letter writers. She makes assignments and 150,000 letters have been sent to congressmen, the President and the hotels. She publishes a newsletter every month. Mary and I sit down and make a course selection based on the most pressing priorities. Mary has made a tremendous impact in this country. She has has been successful in getting Howard Stern off of several key radio stations.

Mary Davis is an amazing person. When she first took a job in a dry cleaners she would not speak. Then she took a college public speaking course and became a speaker. Now she's on the radio, every week, for years. She is constantly feeding and sharing information all over the country. Mary attends Covenant Church, another illustration of churches serving together for a common cause. You overlook your differences and serve a common cause. We stay within the fundamentals of primarily Evangelicalism.

Ashley Nevins is a relative newcomer with a great potential in the homosexual ministry and various addictions. He has been with us three years. Being with CLEAN, and the support he gets from the churches, will propel the homosexual issue into a very prominent position. Modesto has a large number of homosexuals. There are three homosexual bars in Modesto.

Tony Ippolito is another example of unity. He was starting a ministry to homosexual men at one of our local churches. He decided to come under the umbrella of CLEAN so it would not be a particular church, but a community ministry. I think that was a good idea, which strengthened and broadened the ministry.

Bob Herod was a great worker. He was to succeed me as President but he died of cancer. I had a meeting scheduled with him the day he died.

Q. How did God prepare you personally for the unity of the churches? CLEAN wouldn't exist if there were walls, so you have already reaped some benefits from the unity.

A. I told the Board of Directors that started CLEAN to give me 30 days to decide about becoming President. I said, "I will lead the organization if you will give me the support I need." They consented. If the church had said no I would have said No. I wouldn't have taken the leadership.

When I ran for Mayor in 1980, Pastor Yaeger called together twenty six pastors to support my mayorship, which was virtually unheard of. I said to them, "God has revealed to me that we are in for a great spiritual battle in Modesto. There is going to be warfare. Whether I win or lose is not relevant. God has done these things for a purpose." I lost the race, but it imprinted in my mind that here were twenty six pastors doing something unheard of, coming together to support a man. When I saw the twenty six Pastors stand with me as I ran for Mayor and then come together to ask me to be the leader of CLEAN, this was God preparing me for a work of unity in this community.

Q. Were there any bench mark events or statistics in you area of ministry that contributed to the Church of Modesto?

A. We had a rally at Downey High School with former FBI investigator, Bill Kelly, as our speaker. Their auditorium seats 900 people. Not only did we fill the auditorium, but we filled the 400 overflow seats with closed circuit TV in the cafeteria as well. We turned away hundreds of people. When Don Stahl, the District Attorney, saw the outpouring he said, "I was hooked." Don went on to introduce a law which came as a result of CLEAN, that makes a criminal offense a higher degree of penalty if a man used pornography during the act of molestation of a child. It was appealed. The State Supreme Court upheld that decision. It was a great victory. It was broadcast all over the United States to District Attorneys. That was one of the first great things that ever happened.

There was also an event with Judith Reisman. She is very prominent now in the US. There is a bill in Congress to refute Hugh Hefner and the guy that wrote the Kinsey Report on sexuality. She is proving this is a fraud and she wants to debunk the whole thing. She spoke on Donahue. It's the only time I saw Donahue get booed by his own audience.

The other one was Jerry Kirk, a Presbyterian Evangelist from Cincinnati Ohio. He spoke at Neighborhood Church. He directs the National Coalition against Pornography.

Q.   Would you share any victories CLEAN has had here in Modesto?

A.   CLEAN has the distinction of being the only organization to get an anti-pornography bill through legislature since 1968. It was through Gary Condit. It was the bill to put opaque material over the covers of explicit pornographic magazine. It has been accepted throughout the state of California even though it has been challenged.

— Courtesy of Harry Kullijian

Harry Kullijian (right) with District attorney of Orange County, Mike Capizzi, the prosecutor who tried the landmark case in the United States Supreme Court regarding the Miller Decision and Obscenity in 1973.

The big one was when we went to court three or four times on the Adult Book Stores. That is still receiving state-wide recognition for Modesto. This was an issue that people really cared about. When I asked for ten people from each church around Modesto, the courtroom overflowed. We gave each church an opportunity to become involved in the process, and they responded. At the final hearing the judge ruled in our favor. Afterwards I addressed the people and said, "I want you to know that by your presence you have established a standard that you care. Just by coming and standing quietly." Right now we only have one adult book store left in Modesto and it is going to be out of here.

What has happened in Modesto now is that certain attorneys are asking prospective jurors, "Are you a member of CLEAN?" It thrills me to think that attorneys realize if this person is a member of CLEAN they know what this person stands for.

The other issue was sexually oriented businesses. We had four nude dancing bars in Modesto and one in Salida in 1996. Our City Attorney, Mike Millich, because he knew that CLEAN would support him, went to Sacramento several times undercover. He interviewed the managers and dancers. He discovered who the moneymakers were, how and how much money was being made. As a result, an ordinance which established guidelines for nude dancing bars was passed. This became the model for the State of California. Before the ordinance there were seven applications for nude bars pending in Modesto. After the ordinance went through, they withdrew and not one more application was submitted. Rather than prohibiting the business, the ordinance took the profit out of it.

California produces 80-90% of obscenity and pornography in America, primarily in San Fernando Valley, where the 1971 earthquake was centered.

Q.   Why do you think God chose to begin such a work of unity in Modesto?

A. There can only be one answer: because hearts were open, and God knew that in the hearts of men and in the churches of Modesto, His will would be obeyed. It was a "done deal". People's hearts were open and they were willing to rely on God. Most people don't know what relying on God can do in their lives. They want to keep a little bit of control. They don't want to live with reckless abandon. As a result they miss out on what God has in store for them.

Q. Do you see any down side to the unity which is occurring here in Modesto?

A. Not if the churches and GMMA keep their focus on Jesus Christ. The danger would be if they would begin looking at each other or at what they have accomplished. Then there would be a down side. I don't think that has happened.

Q. What lessons or principles have you observed in Modesto which could help other communities bring their churches together?

A. Understanding what discipleship really means. Most people really do not understand discipleship. I've come to understand that it means getting involved with the other person's life. When you become involved in another's life, you and that person are both going to change. I'm speaking of disciplining other Christians. If the Lord isn't allowed to lead, given free reign, then there is no way you can influence or disciple anybody else. God wants to make activists of us all. If we don't give Him free reign to do that, there isn't much fruit, production, activism, or results. It is more an exercise in futility. The end product is fulfillment in our lives.

Another thought is about Christian activism. There is something you can do. I think this is where the key really lies. When we're called, we're absolutely called to the righteousness of God and by faith we respond. That is the whole essence of the activism of the church. I think that individuals who respond to God's call, God uses. Whether it's in the area of poverty, visiting in jail, or serving food, whatever it is, it's the serving of other people as Jesus did at the Last Supper when He washed the feet of His apostles. He said, "I came here not to be served, but to serve." I think that's the whole excitement of being a believer. If you're not an activist, and I mean an activist in the true sense of the word.

Bill Yeager (the former pastor of First Baptist Church) was an activist. The inspiration of Bill Yeager was that he motivated others to be activists. When I say an activist I mean somebody who is actively seeking the will of God and is saying, "What is it You want me to do?" Whether it's service in the church, in the community, in the family, or wherever God is calling you, it is activism! But more importantly, God has called me to be an activist by sharing the Word and by being His disciple in the community. I believe that is the essence of what God has called us to do. If you're an activist, you're going to be an evangelist. It may be that He'll call you to be an evangelist, and that's a possibility. That may be your role, but for the majority of us who are not called to be evangelists, He's going to give us the opportunity to be evangelists through our activism.

C. OBSERVATIONS

1.   CLEAN offers a platform for ministries which local churches who often do not have either the resources or the motivation to operate. Ministries such as those targeting sexual addictions, political action committees, and even hosting special politically focused events offer community opportunities to pool their resources and accomplish goals they couldn't accomplish individually.

2.   Harry Kullijian's decision to accept the leadership of CLEAN was conditional upon the full support of the GMMA. He received it and continues to receive that support to date. The local church community empowers organizations when it supports their purpose, their policies and their leadership.

3.   CLEAN provides neutral territory for church members to gather and serve over a common cause. Its leaders and members represent balanced cross sections of the city's churches.

4.   Unlike most Christian organizations, CLEAN's position is a defensive one. It exists to protect the community from the advances of the enemy in the political arena. These defensive causes have provided rallying points for the Church of Modesto on several occasions.

5.   Genuine Christian activism is to be used as a tool to carry a Christian message into places often left untouched by the Gospel of Christ. As Harry Kullijian put it, "If you're an activist, you're going to be an evangelist"

6.   A political victory is a very powerful event for uniting a community's churches. Conversely, a political defeat may have far-reaching effects on believers. Although the church is not a political entity, it must be aware of the battle that would affect our political freedoms and influence the community either positively or negatively. As such, the church is to be involved in prayer and in support of those leaders who are on the political battlefront.

7.   Modesto is a much more liveable community, for both the churched and the non-churched, due to the leadership of Harry Kullijian and the CLEAN organization. Pornography undermines the health of any community. Organizations which encourage morality and pursue legislation to restrict the influx of pornography in a neighborhood have an impact on the climate of a community and its receptiveness to church influence.

8.   The purpose of a city-wide church is not to focus on political goals such as CLEAN has accomplished. The focus of the COM has always been first and foremost to lift up the name of Jesus Christ. CLEAN represents the work for the Holy Spirit moving in the hearts of individuals within the COM to cooperate as members of one body, rather than separate congregations. They arrived at this point because their primary focus was to lift up the name of Christ rather than a political agenda.

Chapter 8

THE MODESTO
UNION GOSPEL MISSION

A. INTRODUCTION

THE MODESTO UNION GOSPEL MISSION (MUGM) is celebrating it's fiftieth year of service to the community. It had its beginnings in 1948 when Mr. John Haine saw the need to feed the hungry and homeless men for Modesto with food for the body, and the Gospel of Jesus Christ for their souls. Leftover funds from Billy Graham's very first crusade provided the seed money, and Christian businessmen became the first Board of Directors.

The original location on Eighth Street did not provide for shelter. A move was made a few years later to 918 "H" Street where the ministry was located for many years.

As Stanislaus County grew, it became necessary to expand the services available and to begin to include women and children. Facilities for men were moved to the Airport District in 1984, a women and children's shelter opened in 1985, and in 1991 the Mission's warehouse opened to the next level of poor for the distribution of food and clothing.

In 1997 the Mission completed an aggressive $3 million expansion campaign that brought churches, civic organizations, businesses, foundations, and individuals together to address a problem facing communities across America: what do we do with the homeless? New facilities are at 1400 Yosemite Boulevard, still in the heart of the Airport District, one of Stanislaus Counties most disadvantaged neighborhoods.

The MUGM is Stanislaus County's PMU emergency shelter, and is completely privately funded. Over 150,000 meals will be served this year, and almost 2,000 individual men and women, boys and girls will be given shelter. The oldest homeless guest was a ninety-year-old lady whose family put her out on the street in the middle of the night. A police officer brought her to the mission. The youngest was a baby, born in the parking lot faster than the ambulance could arrive.

As society has gotten more complicated, the methods to help people become productive and successful members of society have needed to improve. In addition to the basic needs of food, clothing and shelter, the Mission offers new life programs, education and employment programs, children's safe zone program, medical and dental programs, addiction recovery, resource counseling and referral, spiritual counseling, and a hand of love to everyone who comes for help.

Extensive use of volunteers is part of the Mission's secret to success. Volunteer age groups range from pre-teen to octogenarians. Just like Mission guests, they are also multicultural. They serve food, clean, distribute clothing, tutor, paint, help with children, provide daily devotions, sew, befriend the weary, encourage the weak, and too many other things to list. "Be a Friend to the Friendless" is the volunteer program's motto.

The Modesto Union Gospel Mission epitomizes what can be done when people come together to make a difference.

B. INTERVIEW WITH
DIRECTOR BARBARA DEATHERAGE [18]

Q. Barbara, please give a little of your background and how you are related to the Church of Modesto.

A. My name is Barbara Deatherage. I am the Administrator for the Modesto Union Gospel Mission. I'm actually related to the Church of Modesto because I am a Christian in Modesto. That's really my first affiliation with it. Of course Gospel Missions from their beginning have been a reflection of the Christian community because individually it's very hard to relate to the needs of the homeless. If Christians come together collectively, individual Christians and churches, then a lot more can get done as far as personal resources, different resources that are involved.

I'm from the Fresno area. In the early '70s I moved up to this area. I became interested in the homeless problem at that time. I lived in Vernalis, San Joaquin County. I was most interested in the Stockton Mission.

Q. Were you and Vern were married at the time?

A. No. In 1985 Ferry Morris Seed Company was moving their world headquarters here to Modesto. I sent a resume in to see if there was anything I might be interested in doing because I was ready for a change. I've always worked in Agriculture. I came on board with the seed company here in Modesto, and I moved to Modesto. Vern was living here in Modesto. He and I met and married in 1986. That's when he first became aware of the Gospel Mission. I transferred my love for this type of ministry from the Stockton Mission to the Modesto Gospel Mission, and he fell in love with it too. We started volunteering here. We just got so involved, each of us individually. Vern was a former law enforcement officer and paramedic. He's always been in a protect-and-serve type of job anyway. We just got so involved we each left our individual careers. I was an international credit manager when we left secular work and came here full time, and Vern was in construction.

To make a very long story short, we just really knew God was calling us into this ministry full time. Vern decided to volunteer full time. I was going to support the family. That's the way we were going to start. We had been back east on a business trip for me, taken some days off and really cleared our mind about what was going to happen. When we came back he came in to tell the Director at that time, Jack Hewitt, "I'm going to be here full time." Jack took one look at Vern that Monday morning. Before Vern could say anything, Jack said "Vern, the Lord told me over the weekend you need to work here full time." God just worked it out.

That was in 1989. We had been volunteering since 1986. Jack retired two years later and Vern became the Executive Director. It was just three months after Vern came on staff that the Board asked me if I would come on staff too. It was very interesting. The Mission had never had anybody in Development. It was a step of faith on their part and on our part because our plans had been I was going to support the family. This is not a place where you make a lot of money. But it's been great. We've been part of a miracle here because the Mission at that time was the old fashioned, mom and pop style mission.

Of course, as the Stanislaus County area grew, 39%

between the 1980 and 1990 census, society has become a lot more challenging. When I first got interested in homeless ministry, it was mainly middle-aged or elderly alcoholic men. You could get them dried up, cleaned up, going in a forward motion, and jobs were relatively easy to find. Society was just a lot more simple than now. When I came on board here it was with the intent to expand the ministry and to begin to address the needs in a more expanded way. Vern was the equivalent of the Program Director at that time. He and I were doing totally different things. I was working with Jack and he was working mainly with the program part of it. When Jack retired, Vern became the Executive Director and we really stepped up to another level.

You know this whole concept of the Church of Modesto, the Gospel Mission epitomizes really what happens when a community comes together. Gospel Missions all over the world exist to be an extension and arm of the local Christian community. It epitomizes what can happen when a community comes together to work on a particular project. Individually it's so difficult to meet the needs of the poor. I don't care how big your church is, you can't help everybody who comes. You can't help them in the way they need to be helped. Food, clothing and shelter is, quite honestly, the most simple thing we do. It's all the rest of it. Trying to get them to become functioning members of society and successfully functioning. Of course our number one priority is the Gospel. That's what we are. We are a Gospel Mission, not just a rescue mission.

Q.   How would you distinguish the two?

A.   The old fashioned term of soup, soap and salvation is where the old fashioned missions were. They all

Gospel Mission Directors, Vern and Barbara Deatherage

started out that way. Some missions along the way got more into the soup and soap, and started kind of shoving salvation away. I mean pushing it where it would have, maybe, a secondary role. Where, "Okay, we'll give them the Gospel, but that's not our main function." Here our main function is the Gospel. Because of the Gospel we are able to say that your life can be better. You don't just have life, but you can have it more abundantly. Through discipleship and various programs, tons of programs, we're able to take that next step. But that requires a lot of resources. When you say resources, people seem to think of that in terms of money. Definitely it takes money, but it also takes a lot of human resources. That's where the Christian community also comes in. The Mission itself is a non-denominational, non-profit organization. We are a 501C3. But, we are an inter-denominational work. If you look at the schedule of services, the different churches that come in every night of the month on a rotating basis, there's every denomination imaginable here. When you are talking about people who are coming to help serve food, clean bathrooms, help with the children, so many things are being done here. You can have a group doing the same thing, but they may represent ten different Christian organizations in the area. We epitomize what can be done when people come together with a common cause.

Q.   How did the Gospel Mission contribute to the great sense of unity the Church of Modesto is experiencing today?

A.   I believe that the Church of Modesto really started feeling like it had an identity as the different churches began coming together for prayer. There was a starting point. Of course missions have been around a long time. I would say that we have reaped some benefit from everybody coming together. The Church of Modesto has found its own identity with the tee-shirts, with the rallies, with the Pastors exchanging pulpits, with so many things. Now the Church Community has looked outside of itself to see what else it can do.

We, of course, are an ideal place where you can still come and function as a Christian. You can also function as part of the Church of Modesto while still having your identity in your own church. You can serve the larger community with Christians from other churches. Now that builds community!

Q.   Who were the key people who played a part in your ministry?

A.   John Haine was the first Director of the Mission. It goes back to when Billy Graham had his first crusade in Modesto. The funds from that crusade were used by the Christian Businessmen's Association to start a Gospel Mission. The first Mission was a service and soup kitchen. It has evolved and grown through the years.

There have been various key players through the years. Herb Raske started sheltering people. Bob Lindsey moved the Mission into the Airport District. Jack and Helen Hewitt, who were the Directors before Vern and I, actually came out of retirement when Bob Lindsey died suddenly. They stayed long enough (seven years) for us to come and be trained. We've been privileged to be part of a huge expansion project, a miracle really. Quite a few people through the years have played important roles. The Christian community at large has certainly been a great support.

Q.   Had God done anything in your heart to prepare you
     for this movement of unity?

A.   I believe in order to be involved in a rescue ministry, a
     Gospel Mission, the Lord had to prepare us to be peo-
     ple who could work interdenominationally. The Mis-
     sion, of course, is non-denominational, but the work
     is inter-denominational. The Lord had to prepare us
     already to recognize the church is people. There are
     different houses of worship, different forms of worship,
     but the church is actually the Bride of Christ.

     There was never one particular thing that happened,
     but I do believe that there are people who never see
     that the church is people of different denominations.
     The Mission has a very simple statement of faith, the
     very basis of what makes a person a Christian. Beyond
     that, as regards to forms of worship or interpretation,
     one cannot be concerned with those things when you
     are trying to understand you are part of a very large
     family. For a Gospel Mission to be successful, certainly
     the Directors of that Mission must understand that or
     it would never work. God had to prepare our hearts
     for that.

Q.   Were there any bench mark events or statistics with
     the Gospel Mission which contributed to the Church
     of Modesto?

A.   When we were looking for a consultant to help us with
     the feasibility study of the expansion, we learned we
     could probably raise six to seven hundred thousand
     dollars from the community for this project. Vern and
     I knew this project was necessary and we knew God
     would bless it. It was "supposed" to happen. Even
     though it was one of those things you "had" to do,

we did not care so much what it [the report] said. We were confident God was in the expansion. We trusted God. We knew the greatest challenge was in letting His people know what the need was.

We made sure everybody knew what we were doing, why we were doing it, and how they could be a part of it. God's people responded to the project. They contributed 91% of a three million dollar project. It was a miracle of God! Certainly we were a part of a miracle, but it was because God's people recognized that there was a community need. No one gives to a Mission for their own benefit. They have a roof over their head, food to eat and clothes. They will not be benefitting by what they give the Mission. God has to prompt people to give. Currently, we have 103 area churches supporting us financially on a regular basis. We also have sixty one of the Modesto churches involved in a physical serving ministry of some sort each month.

Homelessness is a community problem. Our community recognized the problem and gave to meet the need. Part of it had to be, I am sure, a result of the Church of Modesto. Not only was this a powerful experience for us to witness, but the consultant, the Board of Directors, and those in the community that knew about it also realized God's hand was involved in this effort. It was a time of affirming that miracles still do happen.

Q.   Why do you think God chose to begin such a work in our city?

A.   When Pastors in our city decided to withdraw together for a certain amount of time to seek God in prayer with no agenda, that had to have been a rallying point or a starting point. God's Word tells us if we draw close to Him, He will draw close to us. That is the only explanation.

We had the privilege of attending a building dedication for the Greater Glory Missionary Baptist Church. When we arrived there were Pastors from five different denominations. That would not have happened before all these leaders began to pray together. They may have been interested and wished each other well, but they wouldn't have attended. It just would not have happened. It was all different denominations. A Presbyterian Minister gave the message in a Missionary Baptist Church! It stemmed from the leaders seeking God, hearing from God, God touching hearts and minds, and knowing that we are a part of the family of God.

Q. Do you see any down side to the unity that is occurring here?

A. I do not believe there is any downside to the unity, but I know there are people who are suspicious of it. Of course, we all know that in the last days there will be a lot of "one world" things, "one church." I believe that has something to do with some of the suspicion that may be there. The whole concept of what makes us Christians, the things that unite us and makes us one family are the only things we are focusing on. No one is trying to change anybody's mind about their forms of worship or some of the other things that make us different.

When you know of all the different Pastors who meet together for prayer on Wednesday, I do not believe there is one denomination that has been left out. I know as we seek God, He continues to straighten these suspicions out. But I cannot imagine a downside because we are seeking God's will, not man's. We are not seeking to build another tower of Babel. We are seeking to have greater communication and empathy for each other and walk with the Lord together instead of separately.

Q. What lessons or principles have you observed here in Modesto which could help other communities bring their churches together?

A. Certainly the principle of having a Ministerial Association is vital. There has to be a rallying point. Within that, someone would need to take leadership, as Dr. David Seifert has done. I know there is also a Board, and that would be important too. I am convinced that leaving town for a prayer summit, where you do not have to answer phones, worry about parishioners or the daily workings of the church and seeking God together, has got to be a good next step. Then, certainly, bringing it back to the community. Not just keeping it to themselves, but allowing us to be a part of it too. I know churches tend to be territorial. I have to laugh at the saying "there are enough sinners for everybody." But if our leaders do not get together this is something that cannot come from the lay people. Sometimes things filter up, but I believe this one has to come from the top.

Leaders in the community will have to take the initial step and not meet just once a month for coffee but to say, "What can we do, how can we pray?" Remember? Our Ministerial Association used to do that. They had a once a month meeting with a program. Everybody was busy, of course, and came flying in and flying out.

But what has given the whole thing lifeblood was when it was decided to do away with the program and make their meetings a prayer time of seeking God, so God blessed it.

As related to the Gospel Mission we are a Faith Organization from the word "go" and have to trust God. We trust Him through His people to meet our needs. Times may change but God never does. As long as that is our guiding light we are in a wonderful place.

C. OBSERVATIONS

1. A Gospel Mission provides a golden opportunity for Christians to serve shoulder-to-shoulder with Christians of other churches. Over sixty churches serve at the Modesto Union Gospel Mission on a regular basis. This grass roots service opportunity develops a city-wide unity at the most fundamental level.

2. The Modesto Union Gospel Mission provided a neutral project for churches to partner together through financial giving. Over one hundred churches give regularly to the Mission. Building projects often have a detrimental effect on members of churches as the push for money becomes a distraction. However, the giving toward this project was met with enthusiasm because the purpose benefitted the whole city. Homelessness is a need felt by almost everyone.

3. People involved in a Gospel Mission have a jump start on unity by the mere nature of their ministry. The ministry reflects physical needs in a community as it addresses the homeless, the financially destitute, the abused, and the rejected. When churches come together to address physical suffering, there is a partnering which occurs, leading to greater unity in other areas as well.

4. The Ministerium's prayer time must not be a business meeting, but a time to do business with God! Prayer must always precede planning. Prayer is foundational to all other activities. It must never be relegated to a quick opening and closing sentence in order to get on with the purpose for meeting. It is the foremost purpose for coming together; to seek the Lord and listen to His direction. The health of an organization can be continually evaluated by the emphasis which is maintained on prayer.

Chapter 9

PROMISE KEEPERS

A. INTRODUCTION

ONE OF THE MOST exciting facets in the life of the Church of Modesto has been the Promise Keepers (PK) movement. The PK California stadium events have provided a visible reference point for all who care to take notice of what God is doing here. From the first California conference in Anaheim in 1994, through the Oakland events and on to the conferences at Bulldog Stadium in Fresno, Modesto's presence has been felt. The greatest single city representation was from Modesto at the 1995 Oakland event with over 5,000 men present. The enthusiasm was inspiring as the men shared a common section of the stadium, as well as a common heritage. The following interview is with Steve Kremer, the Northern California PK representative during those years. He was instrumental in both elevating the visibility and involvement in PK as well as drawing the men of the Modesto area Churches into active participation with his organization and one another across traditional church boundaries.

B. INTERVIEW WITH STEVE KREMER [19]

Q. Steve would you please give a little of your background and how you are related to the Church of Modesto? Also, give a thumbnail sketch of Promisee Keepers

Steve Kremer — "Key Man" in forming the Stanislaus County Task Force for Promise Keepers.

A. I received Christ in September, 1980, and became a member of First Baptist Church of Modesto. I attended there for about four years. I made some poor life choices and walked away from Christ for a while. I was living in rebellion two and one half years before I returned to fellowship with Christ. It was with Pastor Dennis Kazar at Modesto Covenant Church that I recommitted my life in 1989.

In 1994 I became involved with the Singles Ministry at Big Valley Grace Community Church. That year I attended a leadership conference in Sacramento sponsored by Promise Keepers. The men were talking about how God can use us all. My heart was touched. I began to pray about what God would have me do with Promise Keepers.

Q. How did Promise Keepers contribute to the great sense of Unity that the Church of Modesto is experiencing today?

A. When you say the 'great sense of Unity,' you'll just have to hear the story and determine for yourself if we helped.

About 14 of us guys came back from the Sacramento Conference and met at Perko's Coffee Shop in August of 1994. We began to pray and try to determine what God wanted us to do. It was interesting that those fourteen guys represented at least ten different churches. Eventually, we formed the Stanislaus County Task Force for Promise Keepers. In September of 1994, we set a goal to unite the 200 churches in the Modesto Area with what we called the "Key Man" and "Ambassador Network." That was just the beginning of our contribution to the unity.

Q. Who were the key people who played a part in your ministry? What roles did they play?

A.   It would be hard to mention all of the Pastors and key people because there were so many. I will try to mention a few. What you have to understand is that I am an average blue-collar kind of guy. The Promise Keepers is made up primarily of guys like me. I think of Matt Moffett from River Oak Grace Community Church in Oakdale, and Eddie Sai from Turlock, J.R. Selby and Pastor Ross Patterson , Steve Thomas and Bob Rushner from Calvary Temple, Marshall Wheeler from Modesto Covenant, Dan Clipper from Waterford, Steve Hallum and Tony Souza from Big Valley Grace Community Church. There are many, many other guys in addition to these.

As we began to pray, God kept bringing more and more men to our team. We finally had close to 200 Key Men and thirty Ambassadors representing the Stanislaus County Area. Eventually the Modesto Ministerial Association was affected by the movement of the blue-collar leaders. In the Central Valley they could see that lay men wanted to be involved in Ministry in small groups. We also wanted to support and help the Pastors. I think if we played any role, we began to help the Pastors (who are the true leaders in the community) see that we were there to support them. Let me say it again, our role was to support the Pastors. It was always to support the Pastors as well as to encourage men to meet with other men on a weekly basis in some form of an accountability group. The reason that was our goal was that we saw it working for us.

This was a real grass-roots effort. Lay people in the truest sense of the word.

Q.   Had God done anything in your heart to prepare you personally for this movement of unity?

A.   I would say that I had been pretty much an independent, arrogant sort of a guy. I do not think I am unique or unusual in this way as a man. I think most of us men are "Lone Rangers" in that most of us do not have close friends. God humbled me several times in my walk with Him. I didn't have much left with regard to pride and arrogance. I think that's probably when God began to use me. Yes, believe it or not, I finally did have a humble spirit. All I wanted to do was to be used of the Lord. I didn't care in what capacity. I didn't care if I was running a conference or picking up trash, it was all okay. The men that I worked with, the entire task force, had the same servant's attitude. I think that is why God used us. Yes, I'd say God had been giving me a servant's heart.

Q.   Were there any bench mark events or statistics with Promise Keepers that contributed to the Church of Modesto?

A.   The first one I think of was a 'Wake-up Call' we held over at First Baptist Church. It was very interesting. Our goal was to fill up their auditorium, to have one hundred different churches represented. God visited us that evening. We probably had around 2,400 men show up for the event from over ninety churches. It was the first time for Modesto to have this type of large inter-church, Christ-centered event happen. It was spearheaded by the movement of Promise Keepers in our city. That was in February of 1995.

Another bench mark would be the first PK Conference in Oakland. That first conference in June of 1995 was attended by approximately 5,000 men from this area. Because of our attendance, the conference directors gave us special recognition. It was very interesting. Not only Modesto, but Central California was coming together with great momentum at these Conferences. There were probably close to 20,000 men from Central California who attended the Oakland Conference. I would like to also add that the 5,000 men who came from Modesto formed the largest contingent of men to attend from any single city ever.

Q.   Would you share any supernatural experiences in which God demonstrated His handiwork in causing this movement?

A.   There was as Pastors' Conference in Atlanta in 1996 with approximately 45,000 Pastors in attendance. Approximately forty were from the Modesto Area. Another great reconciliation point is that people were reaching out.   Some of the ethnically-diversified churches that did not have the finances for their pastors to get there, were helped.   That is an incredible note in itself.

At that point in time the city of Modesto was gaining national attention for the Ministerial Association and for the Task Force which was bringing the men of the community together. Yes, the Lord was using Promise Keepers to bring visibility to what He was doing in Modesto.

Q.   Steve, would you talk a little about the Volunteers and what God was doing through them.

A.   This was very interesting and exciting. I was asked to be the State Volunteer Coordinator for the Oakland Conference. While in that role the biggest thing I saw happening was that men started getting together, regardless of what church they were from.   They were about Jesus Christ and they were there to serve Him. I see that as a miracle. He was definitely bringing the church walls down through the medium of service to the Body of Christ.

Modesto area Pastors traveled to Atlanta for the 1996 Promise Keeper Pastors Conference. This was the largest representation of any city in America.

Q.   Why do you think God chose to begin such a work in our city?

A.   You know, that is a tough question. I think it has much to do with our pastors meeting once a week for prayer. They really have set a foundation for God to work here in Modesto. From the standpoint of a lay person, I think we just have a desire to meet with other men and grow. The reason why Promise Keepers has grown here so well is that it has created an environment for us to go and have fun together as men, and to be able to understand how Christ loves us. We are just regular guys. We have learned to accept some of the dumb things we do. I guess it's called our humanity. Then to realize that we are not the only ones in this predicament.

Q.   Where do you see prayer fitting in to this movement?

A.   Not only from where the pastors come from, but when we first started the Task Force here in this community, we were bathing it in prayer. That is not at all my style. Sometimes the guys on the Task Force would say, "Listen, let's stop and pray." We did pray and we did fast. God just kept leading us. I am sure it was prayer.

Q.   What lessons or principles have you observed here in Modesto which could help other communities bring their churches together?

A.   For me personally, since I do not have a very good theological background, there were some fears that showed up in my life. I had doubts and fears about God ever being able to use me. Some of the men I worked with felt that way, too. What we need to do is just forget what goes on inside of our heads and listen to Christ.

We also needed to be less critical and not judge other people. I'm telling you, some of the guys who came through to help us on the Task Force were very interesting people. Some I would never have chosen to hang out with. But they were the most faithful servants I have ever met. If God has called you to serve, forget the other stuff and serve. Don't be afraid of the fears that you have. I believe that many times fear keeps us from moving ahead in our lives.

Q. In summary, Steve, I hear you saying to first love each other as Christ loved the church; secondly, eliminate criticism from our lives; thirdly, serve one another; and lastly, move past our fears. Is that accurate?

A. Yes, that is correct.

A. OBSERVATIONS

1. Promise Keepers provided a neutral forum for men from different churches to serve together in a spiritual ministry. This made a natural bridge from individual churches into the Church of Modesto.

2. Lay involvement was where Promise Keepers began and continues to be the strength of the ministry. It has also provided an avenue for lay people to meet, serve, and worship with men from other Modesto churches.

3. Parachurch ministries need not be a threat to the local church or to the cause of community church unity. If parachurch organizations are committed to the local church and purpose to support it in a mutual symbiotic relationship, it can exist.

4.   Having the laymen in a community lead with such a movement of unity is crucial. Men must be the spiritual leaders in the home, the church, and in the community. Effective lay leadership in parachurch organizations often empowers men to more effective lay leadership within the church.

5.   It is probable that the Promise Keeper stadium event provided a model for the Church of Modesto stadium events, which have also been successful in bringing citywide unity.

SECTION FOUR

PARTNERING TOGETHER
IN MINISTRY

"The time is always ripe for re-union. Divisions between Christians are a sin and a scandal, and Christians ought at all times to be making contributions toward re-union, if it is only by their prayers." [20]

C.S. Lewis

The Ministerium leaders have stated repeatedly that the purpose of their efforts toward unity is not to accomplish any great agenda for God but rather to sit at His feet. It is not to work for God but to worship him, it is not to do but to be. The reality of that priority is apparent in the Prayer Summits and Wednesday Prayer Times. Most of their time together is spent in worship activity, and business items are usually reserved for the Ministerium leadership team meetings. However there have been opportunities to minister together as one body in recent years. This section records five such opportunities where the churches have stood shoulder to shoulder in "repairing the wall" as the Israelites did in Nehemiah's day. Those opportunities included the follow up of 52,500 decision cards from the Calvary Temple play, *Heaven's Gates/Hell's Flames*; a gathering for racial unity, a community marriage policy, a youth pastor's network, and a city wide stadium celebration.

Chapter 10

THE MODESTO MIRACLE
A Drama Presentation Entitled
Heaven's Gates and Hell's Flames
presented by
Calvary Temple Church

A. INTRODUCTION

A SOBERING DRAMA depicting the reality of hell apparently has been the sparkplug in a citywide awakening in Modesto, California, a Central Valley city of 176,000, where more than 33,000 people have made professions of faith since January.

Many local Christians believe a four-day prayer summit in early 1994, involving 53 pastors, established the foundation for the revival. But the three-night production of *Heaven's Gates and Hell's Flames* in January at the Modesto Assembly of God Calvary Temple Worship Center served as the catalyst for the large scale revival.

Rudy and Karen Krulik of Reality Outreach Ministries in Niagara Falls, New York, wrote the play and trained Calvary Temple members to act the roles.

Glen Berteau, Calvary Temple's senior pastor, was taken aback by the size of the crowds. "We can seat 2,400, but we had to turn away thousands," he says. When people began standing in line for four hours before performances Berteau determined to extend the drama.[21]

Since this Christianity Today, June 1995, article the drama has been performed annually. Pastor Berteau reports that as of 1999, total of 144,300 people have witnessed the play over sixty three showings. During those performances 55,900 individuals have professed some sort of decision for Christ.

The drama has impacted churches all over town. The follow-up cards have been shared with other churches as those congregations and their pastors were praying for the event. The competitive spirit among congregations has dissipated. Certainly God has used *Heaven's Gates and Hells Flames* to continue the movement of church unity in Modesto as well as reach the lost.

In the following interview, Pastor Glen Berteau shares his perspective on "The Modesto Miracle."

B. INTERVIEW WITH GLEN BERTEAU [22]

Q. Please give a little of your personal background and how you are related to the Church of Modesto.

A. I'm from Baton Rouge, Louisiana. I guess you could say I'm a full blown Cajun, from down in the swamps. I was raised a Catholic. I grew up there, played sports there, and ended up with a football scholarship to Louisiana Tech University. At the end of my junior year I accepted the Lord. My life changed dramatically from then on. I started to work up in North Louisiana, and went to school for a little while. It was then that I got a call from a church in Houston, Texas, to be their youth pastor. I went down there, and got in the ministry and realized this is what God had called me to do. I was in Houston, then I moved to Orlando for four years, and then moved back to Baton Rouge, my home town. Jimmy Swaggart asked me to come to the Jim Swaggart Bible College in Baton Rouge, set up a youth major curriculum there, and to take the youth ministry position. He was just beginning his college. I set up the youth major curriculum and taught in the school. During our four years there it grew to be probably the largest youth ministry in our denomination. We had up to 1,700 on any given Wednesday night. That was at the Family Worship Center in Baton Rouge.

My connection to Calvary Temple was that the pastor here at Calvary Temple, Joe Wright, had two sons he sent to Swaggart's Bible College. Both of them were going into youth ministry. They were both in my classes. As I was training them they were seeing their youth ministry grow. At that time I held two national youth pastor conferences. About 3,000 youth pastors would show up. Joe Wright's youth pastor came to the conference, who happened to be married to his daughter. Four people in his family had been affected, and we were yet to know one another.

Swaggart fell in 1988, and I left that ministry. My wife and I started another church there in Baton Rouge. We stayed there five years, and built a school as well as the church.

Pastor Wright was reaching the point of retirement. I think his kids asked him who would replace him. He said, "I don't know yet." They suggested, "Why don't you get Glen Berteau to come out here?" That was the connection between us, it came through his family.

At the end of '92 I was in Oregon doing a youth convention with a couple thousand kids. Pastor Wright approached me after I spoke one night and said, "I'm retiring. I'm leaving the church." I asked, "Who's taking the church?" and he said, "You're supposed to take it." I said, "Yeah, sure. I'm not supposed to take it."

— Courtesy of Calvary Temple

Glen Berteau, Pastor of Calvary Temple

What's ironic about this is, I have an overhead I did in 1989 with what the Lord was going to do in the '90s. It was sort of a ten-year vision. On that vision I had written a 2,500 seat church on twenty five acres, a prayer chapel, a separate youth and children's chapel, and a training center to train Christians. A lot of things happened and we went through all kinds of attacks. Three years passed and I found myself in this conversation with Pastor Wright. "You're supposed to take my church." I thought, "I'll be nice and listen to this man." I said, "Tell me about your church." He said, "We have a 2,500 seat church, we own twenty five acres, and we have a prayer chapel." I asked, "Where do the children meet?" "They have their own separate sanctuary, and you'll be president of the Bible school." I thought he had read my overhead!

I went back to the hotel, and I asked, "God, what are you saying?" He said, "I don't want you to have to build all that. I wanted to give it to you. You've been through enough."

We came out here and preached a couple times. I didn't need a job. I wasn't preaching for a job. I couldn't see myself, being an old southern boy and my wife being from Louisiana, in California. To people in the East, California is like another country, a foreign country. I never thought in a million years this is where God would send us, but He did. We prayed about it, we preached, and I went back and still was not convinced. God just kind of woke me up one night and He said, "Joe Wright was to build the building, you're supposed to fill it. I want you to go there. I don't want you to take anybody with you because you're going to need a level of ministers that are able to handle a revival." I came here. Yes, I was definitely called here.

When I came to this area, I didn't know anybody. I didn't know any pastors. I didn't know anything that was going on locally. I just knew that God called me to come to this city. My vision has always been city. I've

Calvary Temple's Sanctuary, home of "the Modesto Miracle".

never come to build a church in any place. I've come
to affect a city for Christ. When I came to this city it was
God who brought me here, to see revival take place
in this town. I was unaware of any meetings. I just
knew there was a divine purpose in God bringing me
to Modesto. Out of all the places I know, why here?
I remember several phone calls from friends of mine
asking, "Where are you now Berteau?" I answered,
"I'm in Modesto." "Where's Modesto?" You always
have to pull out Gallo Winery. "Have you ever heard
of Gallo Winery?" Because everybody's heard of it. I
would say, "Their home office is here in Modesto." I
got tired of talking about a winery as what this city is
known for. The Bible speaks about a new wine that
God wants to pour out.

I remember praying and fasting, and I asked, "God, why Modesto? Why did you bring me here?" I've worked in major cities. I was in Houston, Texas; Baton Rouge, the capital of Louisiana; in Orlando, Florida, but now I'm in Modesto. I asked, "Why Modesto? What's going to happen in this place?" He said, "Had you heard of Lynchburg, Virginia, before Falwell went there?" No. He said, "What about Virginia Beach. Was that any big deal before the 700 Club was established there?" No. He said, "Have you ever thought that probably the number one seller of worship tapes distributed throughout the world would be based in Mobile, Alabama? Hosanna Integrity." I said, "No, you'd think it'd be Nashville." He said, "It's in Mobile, Alabama. Remember that? Did you ever think that one of the greatest revivals in this century was named after a street called Azusa? Why not Modesto? You have forgotten I take obscure places and I put them on the map, and this is what I'm going to do." Before I ever knew of any vision of any pastor in town, I already had a vision of what God wanted to do, but not to the magnitude of the first drama night.

Q.   Glen, would you talk about the drama and your preparation for it?

A.   When I first came here I preached for about a year to set our church up for what I felt was going to take place. I knew that God was going to use this drama, but not to the extent it happened. The scripture in Habakkuk 1:5 says, *"Look among the nations, and watch, and be utterly astounded, for I'll do work in your days that you would not believe though it were told you."* God just spoke to my heart and said, "If I tell you what's going to happen, you wouldn't believe Me." That's what the

— Courtesy of Calvary Temple Assembly of God

Throngs coming to Christ at *Heaven's Gates & Hell's Flames.*

scripture says, *"You would not believe though it were told you."* And who would have believed me? Say I'm sitting in a meeting with pastors, and I say, "You know what guys? In twenty eight days, 33,000 people are going to get saved." They might think, "Oh ho, little chosen dreamer with your colored coat. Thank you for sharing your little dream with us, and we want to kill you." It just was not going to fly. It was kind of crazy and so idealistic. I could hardly believe it. I don't think anybody else would have believed it.

I remember my associate had about 300 follow up packets prepared. Like, "We've got a little three-day thing." Now I believed for more than that. The first night of the drama we had 800 people saved. We didn't know where to put them. We had our classrooms set up and they were full. The next night it was 1,000. Then the third night, 1,200.

The drama was entitled *Heaven's Gates and Hell's Flames*. It deals with different aspects of life such as when people die and where they spend eternity, heaven or hell? One part of it is the separation that will take place between loved ones when one is saved and the other is not. One makes it to heaven and one makes it to hell. It really makes you think. You wonder why would so many lost people would want to watch something like this, but there is a real anointing on it. This drama has been going on for sixteen or seventeen years. It isn't something brand new thing that all of a sudden has hit the scene.

Several years ago the founder's wife had a vision of people standing hours in line trying to get into the drama. When it broke out here, they flew in from Canada. When they drove up and saw the lines, she was seeing exactly what had taken place in her vision. Four hours before the doors opened, people were coming in. Others were tailgating, spending nights here, barbecuing in the parking lot.

The last night 1,200 people were saved at the altar. I stopped it. I stopped it because I did not necessarily feel we were called to be a revival center. People now were coming from Oregon, Arizona, and from different states. We had established this but I felt the responsibility on the pastoral side of me to ask where are these people going to go to church? We've got to get their names. At the altar call I would say, "When you're filling out your cards, write down the name of your church if you're affiliated with any."

Q.   How did the drama contribute to the great sense of unity that Modesto is experiencing today?

A.   I think this is what happened. Possibly there were feelings like, "Who's the new boy in town and why is he seeing a revival?" But then who are we to question the way God does things anyway. God chooses to pour out His blessings on who He wants to. That's not our choice.

We had all these different church names that were written on the salvation cards. We were spending most of the day packing salvation information packets to get ready for the night ahead. These cards were just an avalanche on us. We sent the cards to the churches listed and told them these are people who have been saved at the drama. It wasn't long before we had churches calling us back. At one of the Baptist churches, we heard that twenty five people were baptized, the most they ever had baptized at one time. We had another church say they had doubled in attendance and had gone to two services. "Don't send any more cards because we don't have any more room". We had many comments like these. I think now, when we look back, we realize how many people are in our churches and have become part of all our ministries from the drama.

Since then we have had, because of that one out-reach, 52,500 people saved. As Ed Silvoso has said, "If you've got a place like this, thank God for it, because they're not all going to one church. They're going to settle in every church in town." Thank God there's somebody. As Ted Haggard's book, Primary Purpose says, we're raising the water level. If every boat that's on the water rises with it, then I think every church in town gets blessed by it, which is not a problem with me. The whole point is just to reach people in the city. What Ed Silvoso is speaking about is what we did four years ago and it is changing the climate. You do that by adding more Christians.

We present the drama once a year. We'll do it again this next year and I believe that we'll pass out all the tickets. We get the unity of the pastors ahead of time. They start pushing it because they all have people who have not been to the drama. If we now activate all this and combine it with the prayer walks, and then start passing out tickets, God will continue to bless our efforts. We've had 130,000 come through the doors in fifty seven nights. But we still have not saturated the city. The potential is still here in this situation. Yet some may never come to get saved at this. However, more have been saved here in as short a period of time than any place I've ever heard of.

This has really become an evangelism tool for all of the Modesto churches, because they don't all stay in our church. Basically, it's almost like we're just housing the thing here, setting it up and presenting it, because they come from all churches. We had Big Valley Grace Community Church this year bring 250 from their junior high school. Three fourths of them came forward.

They felt like they needed to make sure that this was right and it was a great time! It was wonderful! Let them see it

Q.   Who were the people who played a key part in the ministry here? What roles did they play? This is kind of a unique situation, but you might want to mention the name of the drama people.

A.   Rudy and Karen Krulik oversee this thing. They're from Niagara Falls, Canada. They just send a director while all the actors are our own people playing the parts. They're not professional actors. What people don't realize is the amount of prayer and fasting that goes forth before they ever arrive. We may do a twenty-one-day fast, and at times we have done forty days. Our whole church will take days, segments, and at times we have hundreds of people fasting. Gap-standing prayer has to take place as well. It's as Silvoso says, we must go out and bless people. Yes, we're praying for people. We have thousands of cards and names laying on our altar for weeks. They are seen by the people at every service when they walk in. We pray for them at every service. It's not like, "Well you guys got lucky." No, there is a lot of effort and organization to see something like this happen. It still may not happen even after you do it because it's God's choice. But I at least want have the platform to say, "God we've at least done everything we could, at least what we know to do. If you decide to move, we don't want to obstruct it. We want to allow Your flow."

Q.   Glen, had God done anything in your heart to prepare you personally for this movement of unity?

A. As I shared in my testimony, God was preparing me for both the play as well as the unity movement. As far as the growth, we grew a good bit before the drama ever came. It's just kind of continued. It's just been God's favor, He has just given us His favor and we thank Him for that. We're very humble because you realize what has happened is so beyond you, you don't want to let go of what God has done. It breaks you to where you're very careful to not allow pride to come in.

Q. Would you share any supernatural experiences or life stories where God demonstrated His handiwork through *Heaven's Gates and Hell's Flames*.

A. I'll give you one from this years drama. Here is a ritual knife used to do occult rituals where you cut your wrist and cut parts of your body. It is little so you can carry it and conceal it. The ritual knife was brought up by a gal on a Tuesday night. At the end of the evening, some people had come up to me and said that we have something to put in the bag. One man put in a thing with a patch of the black sun. The black sun is an occult symbol which is the opposite of what Christ would be, Light. Then his wife put in the ritual knife. When I asked her what it was, she said, "It's a ritual knife. I've cut myself many times through rituals and blood sacrifices to the devil." I gave them a talk on all the paraphernalia, and told them to get it out of their house. My wife, who is an intercessor said, "Glen, are you going to pray for them?" I was thinking, here's two people who have been in the occult. I have prayed for many people who have been demon possessed before and seen manifestations. If you will read the new testament, in many of Jesus's meetings demons cried out. I knew that if I prayed right now for these people, right on this platform, there's going to be a manifestation because these people are full blown in the occult. My wife didn't care that there might be a scene. She said, "Glen, we've got to pray for them before they leave. We can't let them go like this." The lady's eyes were twitching. When she looked, they were like nervously twitching. You could tell there was a possession there. My wife starts praying and just touches the lady on the head. The lady falls out. Remember, they've never been to church before and they don't know what falling out or anything is. They've never seen it. Then I touched him on the head. He falls flat out on the floor and he's out. Well, these folks were delivered from Satan's hold that night. It was a dramatic deliverance as God demonstrated His power over the enemy right there on the platform for all to witness.

Other testimonies: [23]

I am a school bus driver. I have over seventy high school students on my bus. I had invited all of them to this *Heaven's Gates and Hell's Flames* drama. Over half came and gave their hearts to the Lord. One of my boys got on my bus the next morning after coming to the program and gave me his blue rag. He said he was out of the gang and was bringing the rest of his "homies" (gang) to the *Heaven's Gates and Hell's Flames* that night. He brought them all. The whole gang are now saved, born-again Christians. Over half of my students are now saved.

Bus Driver

My life seemed over; I was depressed because of the mess I had made of my life. I started reading the Bible. I wasn't raised in church. God led a Christian to ask me to see *Heaven's Gates and Hell's Flames.* I knew I had to go, but I was nervous. I went to the play and said the sinners prayer with the construction worker in the play and received Christ at that time. A life of drugs and sin is gone. Now I have no craving to take drugs again. I had never been able to kick that. Praise God!!!

R.S. - Modesto

About two months before the drama, I was in a place with my walk with God where I wanted to know He was real. I read in the paper of the play *Heaven's Gates and Hell's Flames.* After fighting the crowds and the rain, I finally saw the play (nine times). My family is quite large and because of the drama, six of my family have been saved. My sister told a friend and 12 members of that family have been saved. I am sure that this story can be told by many families. Probably only eternity will reveal the complete effects on the city of Modesto and the surrounding communities.

A.F. - Modesto

Q.   Glen, why do you think God chose to begin such a work in our city?

A.   I guess because He's God. He does what he wants, where and when he wants. I think also because we have been praying in this city. Prayer has been a part of everything we have done here at Calvary Temple as well as a big part of the ministerial meetings.

Q.   Do you see any down sides to the Church of Modesto movement?

A.   No, none that I can see.

Q.   What lessons or principles have you observed here in Modesto which could help other communities bring their churches together?

A.   After our experience here at Calvary Temple I would encourage other churches to use the drama as well. Obviously, there is no guarantee that God is going to move in the same way He did here, but I do recommend it. I also would encourage other communities to work together on evangelism and follow up like we have here.

C. OBSERVATIONS

1. The cooperative follow-up effort of the *Heaven's Gates and Hell's Flames* events were not planned by the church leaders. The cooperation was a reaction to the overwhelming response of the people to God's Spirit. When God wants us to move us in a new direction or cause us to work together, He can make it happen. In addition to cooperation was the absence of a competitive spirit in the Modesto churches. This made for fallow ground for the Holy Spirit to reap a great harvest through this crusade.

2. God uses the foolish things of this world to confound the wise. The drama used untrained players from the local church, not a highly skilled traveling drama team. He wants and deserves all the credit for revival.

3. Prayer was the foundation for this movement of God's Spirit. Prayer from not just Calvary Temple, but the entire Christian community and pastors.

4. One great spiritual victory can build confidence, assurance and unity. As Glen Berteau writes in the account of HGHF: "We had seen it and we knew it could happen again. If God could save thirty-three thousand people using a drama about heaven and hell in a church located in an agricultural city during the space of forty-seven days and twenty-nine performances, He could do anything." [24]

Chapter 11

MEETING AT THE TRACK
A Step Toward Racial Reconciliation

A. INTRODUCTION

Prayers, Hymns at Railroad Unite Christians Under God
by Patrick Giblin *Modesto Bee* Staff Writer

SOME SAW the gathering as a unification among Christians. Others saw it as the first step to break down cultural, racial and economic barriers.

Whatever the view, the first prayer gathering at the tracks Saturday morning attracted several hundred people. Not even a 10:30 am train could spoil the mood.

A few called the event "Mo Church."

The idea sprung forth from a weekly prayer meeting held by several dozen Modesto area church leaders, said Brad Hawn, pastor at First Baptist Church. The pastors pray for each other for about an hour. Hawn said the suggestion came up to expand the prayer meeting into a prayer session for the community. "I've been praying with the pastors for a couple years and it's been exciting to see this all come together," Hawn said. "Here we can concentrate on what we agree on. That's Jesus Christ. He died for our sins."

The railroad crossing between Eighth and Ninth Streets at H Street was chosen as the symbolic meeting place of east and west Modesto.

Most of the people at Saturday's meeting heard about it through their churches. More than a dozen congregations were represented.

A few minutes after 10:00 am, several pastors gave short speeches and led the more than 500 people in prayer and song.

Darius Crosby, pastor at the Progressive Missionary Baptist Church, told the crowd that no courtroom in Los Angeles or differences in opinion should keep Christians apart. Those who share belief in Jesus, he said, should not be divided.

"This is awesome," said Darrel Williams, who was among those who attended. "This is needed to break down the barriers of denominations and racial division."

To symbolically break down those barriers, volunteers held up long ribbons on each side of the track. The idea was to cut the ribbons and allow people from both sides of the track to come together.

A Southern Pacific train had other ideas. Before the ribbon could be cut, a freight train slowly rolled in and split the crowd for nearly five minutes.

"This is typical of Satan's tribe to steal the thunder of what we are trying to do today," Rob Dooley said.

Others saw it more as an intervention by God who demonstrated the physical and cultural reality of the world we live in.

"The tracks have divided us all these years," Dan Peterson said. "One big church was the idea today and not even a train can stop it."

After it passed, the ribbon was cut and the crowd gathered on the west side of the tracks and started a mile-long march to the Progressive Missionary Baptist Church on Fourth Street.

That church is next to a boarded-up house covered in graffiti and across from the Westside Park, described by several neighbors as a haven for drug dealers.

"I don't think I had ever walked that part of town before", said the Rev. Paul Hallock, pastor at the Living Water Bible Church.

There they gathered on the front lawn and in the street in front of the church, prayed, sang more songs, and heard a few more speeches. Neighbors came out and joined the crowd.

"At first I thought there was going to be a big riot," Fourth Street resident Ron Hopkins said, "but then I heard the singing and I thought, 'Thank God. This is fantastic.'"

Hopkins' wife, Diane, agreed, "Maybe this will slow down some of the gangs around here," she said. "I see a lot of the neighbors are out. Maybe if this starts inside the home, we can clean up the neighborhood."

B. INTERVIEW WITH REVEREND DARIUS CROSBY, SENIOR PASTOR [25] OF GREATER GLORY MISSIONARY BAPTIST CHURCH

Q. Darius, would you please give a little of your background and how you are related to the Church of Modesto?

A. I was originally from Monroy, Louisiana. I came to California in 1973, at thirteen, with my father, who was a pastor.

I made a profession of faith at fifteen years. I attended high school in South Los Angeles, and college at Fresno State where I received a degree in journalism. I worked as journalist for eight years prior to entering ministry. During those formative years, I had a few traumatic experiences that directed me into a ministry of racial reconciliation.

My first incident occurred at fourteen years of age. I was sitting across a street on a bicycle. I had a toy pistol or cap gun in my hand. Two large white police officers walked up to me and began joking about my "firearm." One was joking but his partner started using profanity and said, "That's not a toy, that's the real thing." I had members of my family in law enforcement and there was a big deal about honor. This profanity to a kid shocked me. The cop said, "Matter of fact, get up and give me your weapon." It was a game I didn't really understand. He began to get really belligerent. I was giving him the gun. He began to put his thumbnail into my hand and then to put my hands behind my back. To make a long story short, an all out struggle occurred between he and I. His partner didn't quite know what to do. He wrestled me down to the ground and a mob of people came out. I'll never forget the cop pulled a gun on a neighbor named Terry who had served in Vietnam and said, "If you come any closer, I'll blow your head off". Then my mother came running up and the guy told her the same thing. I thought I was going to lose my mom there cause she kept coming. But he didn't shoot her. They put me into the back of the police car and beat me up. They whisked me off. I never will forget one of the officers turning around and saying, "Don't you ever embarrass a white cop on the street like that again." He called me some racial slurs. When we arrived at the station I understood why I was there. My mother found out where I was, entered the station and demanded that they let me go. He said, "He has hurt himself. We need to call an ambulance." My mom said, "No, I will call it myself." But the police had surrounded the project where I lived and they sent the ambulance away three times. Finally one of the neighbors said, "Call a private ambulance." So a private van was let in and that is how I got to West Adams Hospital.

The very next year I accepted Christ. Even though I had been raised in a Christian home I had to make that personal decision on my own.

This incident served as a catalyst and motivation behind the meeting at the tracks. In my mind, its a black and white thing. Whites don't like us and we don't like them. Even after becoming a Christian and getting to meet some other Christians who were white, their attitudes were such, not like that person really knew Christ. I still had that struggle.

After high school I went to Fresno State on a journalism and track scholarship, and excelled there. I sat out my last year of eligibility of track and field to focus on some of the things I felt the Lord was doing in my life. One day I ran into one of the members of the track team, a hammer thrower between 6'3" and 6'4", 265-270 pounds. "Hey, you are no longer on the team. We need your suit back." I asked the guy, "Did the coach send you to get the suit?" He said, "No, I appointed myself. You think you're so smart," and he goes on with all this stuff. He confronted me in front of the gym, kicked me in the groin. A struggle broke out and the police responded. We have a recorded conversation of the phone call to the police. "There's a black guy over here who appears to be on drugs and is causing problems." The police showed up and I thought, "Good, I'm going to get some help here." However, instead the police jumped in, put a choke hold on me, beat me nearly unconscious, and threw me into the back of the police car. The police treated the perpetrator like a victim and they were laughing with him. I could hear the guys at the campus police station using profanity, laughing saying "This guy must be on drugs to try to pick on a big guy like that." They treated me like a druggie, a troublemaker. From there I went to the Fresno County Jail. I stayed in jail for three days and was charged with assault and battery

Pastor Darius Crosby with Y.F.C. director Rick Fritzmeyer — Former teammates on Fresno State track team — now on the COM team.

on this weight lifter and the two policemen. I was facing a fine of $20,000 and ten years in prison. When I finally managed to talk to my coach, he pleaded for my case.

A lot of things had happened to make me think the blacks are on one side and the whites are on another. That's just the way it was. Dealing with Christian people who also shared those views made it much more difficult for me to see it differently. Then the Lord did something for me. I sang in the choir at the John Wesley Church. When I came up for arraignment and saw the courtroom packed with white people from church supporting me, the Lord began to speak to me. It was so packed they opened up the door and they were out on the quad. I had never seen anything like this.

The Lord said, "You think this is a black and white issue? I am going to exonerate you and there will not be one black on the jury." I said, "There are no blacks on the jury? They are never going to clear me." I still remember the District Attorney's words. She said, "You've seen people like this. You have to put them away for awhile." My attorney fought to keep as many blacks on the panel, but all of them were removed. Finally, there were two Mexican-Americans, one Asian and nine whites left. After twenty two appearances I was exonerated. I still remember the judges words. "The defendant Darius Omega Crosby is hereby exonerated and must be immediately released".

From that experience I took an immediate step into ministry. From that point I knew God called me into a ministry of reconciliation.

After working as a journalist for eight years and attending seminary, I received a call to come to Modesto to be a pulpit conductor. There, for the first, time I saw in black people some of the very prejudices that I saw in white people. There were some who would be happy if white people stayed on their side of town. I couldn't understand how that could be a character in people of faith. That really bugged me.

During that time I met Charlie Crane. Charlie brought me to the ministerium and I met many of the pastors. When I met all those white, Mexican and Asian pastors finally I started thinking back to when I was a small kid in Louisiana; every town which track and field or journalism had taken me, even Venezuela, something was constant. They all had railroad tracks which separated people racially, socially, economically, and politically. Even as a small boy the tracks separated me from white boys. You couldn't go across the tracks to play with them.

One day the Lord called my attention to those railroad tracks. The Lord spoke to my heart, that He wanted to do something different at the tracks besides people throwing stones at each other. He began to make that the hallmark of reconciliation.

I'm often asked the question, "Why all this about blacks and whites?" My reply is: "When foreigners come to this country, they determine how they are going to treat me as an African-American on the basis of how 'white America' treats me." If I am neglected in that relationship, it has been my experience that this is the way they have learned to treat me because of what they learned from whites. I believe blacks and whites will set the tone for the relationship between the races. You must do something first between the blacks and whites because it will lay a foundation of reconciliation for all races.

This has been my cry since entering the ministry. We have unfinished work to do. It is a priority. You cannot do well in other things until you deal with the unfinished business. I can pretend I have my work done. Even if no one calls me on it, I know deep down inside that I have unfinished work."

Q.   Darius, please give a thumbnail sketch of the Meeting At The Tracks.

A.   One night at a Bible study at the church where I pastored, I began to tell the people about my idea for a Meeting At The Tracks. I saw different races coming together, praying, walking together to a church, and having a meeting together. They began to tell me how impossible it would be. Modesto is not really a friendly town. The white people have been doing their thing for years. I mentioned this was not my idea but the Lords. I didn't get a whole lot of support, just a sprinkling. But once we got in touch with the police chief and talked about traffic, I began to get some more support from black pastors in the area. Soon everyone was responsive. Even the local TV station, KNSO, who shot a segment. A train came through and symbolized division, and then we talked about reconciliation. People were leaders in the way the Lord wanted them to be.

Close to 2,000 people walked from the center of Modesto where the first part of the celebration was held, walked to the tracks, cut the ribbon, prayed, and the train came. A lot of things happened there, hugs, handshakes, tears. We talked about the symbolism of the train and the tracks. I think somewhere in my speech I talked about there are no tracks in heaven.

Then the group marched over to the west side of town, the "black" side of town. There were white families that walked together. You could hear people saying, "I haven't been here in twenty five years. We have to do this again."

I personally had hoped the place would be flooded by a lot more African-American people. The Lord told me, "It is important for your black brothers to be here, but be satisfied. I need to get these white brothers over here first." He said, "You can't measure success by people's responsiveness. Be content".

Q. How did the Meeting At The Track contribute to the great sense of unity the Church of Modesto is experiencing today?

A. From my experience, there are quite a few pastors and members of churches that trace their involvement in and their acknowledgement of the Church of Modesto to the Meeting At The Tracks. I was with an individual not long ago who said, "My involvement began with the meeting at the track." Some people were inspired by the symbolism of walking across the track and the great changes that took place. It heightened their awareness and involvement in the Church of Modesto, and improved their commitment to the unity of the church. It also gave minorities a better sense of the sincerity of our white brothers and sisters.

A statement was made that God had really dealt with the Church of Modesto because of His concern that an African-American was leading this meeting at the track. He said how good he thought it was that white Christians actually followed a black leader in this thing. He had feared it would not take place.

Q. Who were the key people who played a part in the meeting at the track?

A. As Chairman of the GMMA, Dave Seifert was the very first person I shared this vision with. It was a brief statement, but he got behind it. I believe he encouraged other brothers to as well. He probably wouldn't even consider that he did, but he is highly respected and is a man of integrity. If he put his signature on it, I think people were more willing to embrace it.

Wade Estes played an important role, too. I got to know him in a way I had not known him when we went to the Promise Keepers Pastors Conference in Atlanta. Wade gave me that sense of encouragement that whatever God wanted to do, he was going to be there to support me. He always communicated that he was for what God wanted.

Q.   Had God done anything in your heart to prepare you for this movement of unity?

A.   During my whole life God was preparing me for this Meeting At The Track. There were certain mentors in my life that helped prepare me for this. One of the things was in the Second Baptist Church of Merced. There I saw a predominantly black church feed needy white people every Wednesday at noon. To me that was an event where God said, "Look. This goes both ways. This is not just a black and white issue of racism. This is a spiritual matter."

Q.   Were there any bench mark events or statistics that contributed to the area unity? Do you know how many black churches there are in Modesto?

A.   There were an estimated 2,000 people at the Meeting At The Track. That was a very good start. A majority of them were white. This event was designed solely for the purpose of building unity, racial unity.

I think there are twelve Baptist churches. There are six or seven other churches, but I'm not sure of their denominations. Maybe a few more tiny ones. Perhaps 20 black churches in Modesto.

The population of Modesto is 180,000; 6.5% to 7% are African-American, with fourteen to sixteen total African-American churches.

Q.   Why do you think God chose to begin this work of unity in Modesto?

A.   One of the first things a person might gather is this town is ready. It is unified. They have gone into the "upper room" and prayed. The truth is, however, Modesto has had a history just like any other town. It has not been free of racism or struggles. If you talked to some of the African-American pastors that have been in town for any length of time, they can tell you about battles they have experienced. A lot of the racial prejudices have been covert. People have moved in Modesto. We are like any other city. We do have a racial past. When God moves in the hearts of people, miracles can happen. The Church of Modesto is a reflection of God's work.

Q.   Would you share any supernatural experiences?

A.   I believe the response of the white churches was a miracle. Also the support of the Police Department when they escorted the parade of people both to and from the Seed's of Joy Church where we had our service.

One special thing for me regarding the Meeting At The Tracks was the TV story the 700 Club did. That was really encouraging!

Do you see a down side to the Church of Modesto? Some have said that the GMMA is run by large, white churches. Do you share that concern?

Because of the vision and acceptance of the call to pastor by the brothers in the Church of Modesto, I have been a benefactor. Certainly we have not achieved all we would like to in our efforts for unity. But you are not going to hit a home run every time you get up to the plate. We need to remain faithful and time will iron out some of the concerns people have expressed. For myself, I have no reservations.

Q. Are there any lessons or principles you have observed here in Modesto that could help other communities?

A. Usually the size of the church and the "status" of the pastor determines who his friends are going to be. What has happened in Modesto is that pastors from large and small, predominantly white churches are developing friendships with pastors from different races, different denominations, and different church sizes. That is something occurring here which could help other cities. People look for their comfort circle. We can now refer people to a church on the basis of the truth being taught there. We used to say, "You're black and you don't look like you have much money. I know a church that is black and doesn't have much money." We won't say that to a person, but we often think like that. A guy comes in with a three-piece suit on, looks upwardly mobile and you send him to a wealthier church. I've seen that happen in the past. Now we invite people to the Church of Modesto rather than our own church. We are hospitable in the local church, but we are not hustlers or recruiters. God has blessed the Church of Modesto as a result.

C. INTERVIEW WITH CHARLIE CRANE, [26]
PASTOR OF GREATER TRUE LIGHT CHURCH

Charlie Crane is a pillar within the GMMA, the fact that he is black and not caucasian makes his presence in the organization doubly significant. His faithful presence and timely words of wisdom at meetings demonstrate a deep commitment to racial harmony and even more to unity within the Body of Christ. Charlie's comments on the Meeting At The Track as well as the general state of racial harmony within the Church of Modesto are extremely valuable.

Q.   Charlie would you introduce yourself and tell how are you related to the Church of Modesto?

A.   My involvement in the Church of Modesto stems from my involvement at First Baptist Church.   They invited me in while I was involved at the Second Baptist Church. In 1972 I joined First Baptist Church. It was an all-white church and I am black. The racial thing was a hinderance to me because I thought I would not be accepted.   However, I was accepted there and became one of the interns while I was going to seminary. In 1976 there were about twenty five men on staff at First Baptist Church. Pastor Yaeger and Pastor Blanc, the pulpit pastors, were both going to be out town.   Pastor Yaeger asked me if I would bring the message in his absence.   I asked him what I should speak about. He said, "Anything that is on your heart." To me that was my full acceptance into First Baptist Church, the intern program and into the ministry.   This man with 4,000 members in his church turned to me with full trust that I would speak from the Lord. Since then I have been involved with the GMMA and all the people involved because of Pastor Yaeger.

In 1979 I finished Mennonite Biblical Seminary and was offered a position at First Baptist Church. I did not feel I was needed there. I went to the Westside of town with my wife and founded Greater True Light Baptist Church. I was ordained by Pastor Yaeger. First Baptist really came along side of us as a sister church and co-signed for us to buy the building we are now in. They stood by us while we got on our feet. We have been there eighteen years now.

Q.   Let's talk about the Meeting At The Track. How did it contribute to the sense of unity in the Church of Modesto?

A.   The Meeting At The Track was intended to move the invisible wall that separates the Westside from the rest of the city. The railroad track had always stood for separation. Not only racially, but economically. Not just in Modesto, but in most cities. The point of meeting at the tracks was to solve in our hearts that no longer would there be a separation racially or economically, but we would be one body of believers. I feel the Meeting At The Track was a start in that direction. In truth, the walls are not completely down yet, but we are moving in the right way.

Our Wednesday prayer times meet at First Baptist Church because it is the most central location. But I don't think there will ever be 100% participation from the Westside because of several reasons: the size of First Baptist Church and who is running the program. Big churches usually receive all the attention and recognition, and swallow up the little churches. One of the first things the minority pastors want to know is, "Who is calling the shots?" "Who is running

Pastor David Seifert with Pastor Charlie Crane of Greater True Light Church following a Wednesday Pastor's Prayer time.

the program and whose idea is it?" They have seen enough programs come and go. They don't want or need another program. Small churches often have the feeling of being second- class citizens.

Governments can give us programs without changing hearts, and we continue to feel like second-class citizens. The church is the only one who can make us feel like equal citizens. By that I mean individuals within the church. The only time the church can do that is when they focus on Jesus Christ and are willing to suffer the way He suffered.

The first thing we need to do is what Paul said, "Think more highly of each other than ourselves." When we returned from the first Pastors' Prayer Summit, we said that we were not going to spend our prayer time recognizing each other's programs. We were going to spend it in prayer. Sometimes I fear we have slipped a little bit on this commitment and recognize programs which are deemed worthy of recognition. However, it seems the only programs worthy of recognizing are from the large churches. The reason is their size gives them the ability for technology, publicity, resources, and big names. If you start calling attention to the big players, you lose the little people. If you spend 15 minutes of prayer time promoting a program like *Heaven's Gates and Hell's Flames*, as good as it is, you will lose half your people. Then the "little guys" feel like they've been brushed aside. They can't compete.

Q.   Had God done anything in your heart to prepare you personally for this movement of unity?

A.   I remember years ago when the ministerium met in different churches each month. We really weren't doing much other than going to meetings. Right after the first Prayer Summit it seemed things started to happen as far as people coming together, churches recognizing the ministry of other churches, and recognizing that God gave us different gifts for different reasons. When Ted Haggard was here he discussed the Ephesians 4 passage and suggested different churches have different gifts. No one has a monopoly on God. I used to have the "Elijah Complex." "Here I am. All the prophets are dead and here I am all by myself." I had no one to turn to and pray with, or share my sorrows with until this thing started to come together. Then I found out I could call others. It is really encouraging. It is almost like God saying, "Hey, I have other people in this city, you're not out there all by yourself." I found a new hope in the people of God."

Q.   Have you seen any supernatural acts or the hand of God move in Modesto?

A.   Some of the greatest experiences for me were the Prayer Summits. It was a time when God brought us together. We got to know each other, prayed for one another and joked together. God showed us how much we had in common. For me, it has been at the Prayer Summits where the walls really began coming down.

Q.   Why do you think God chose to begin such a work of unity in Modesto?

A.   In I Corinthians we read God likes to take the weak things of the earth and shame the strong. He picked the "ugliest" city around to shame the others. It's humorous when you think of it. I think there are a lot of Christians in Modesto. Maybe because there is a higher percentage of Christians here than in other cities.

Q.   What lessons or principles have you observed here in Modesto which could help other communities bring their churches together?

A.   The only principle I can think of is humility. When we can stop trying to "save face," go to one another and say, "Let's pray together," I think that is the right place to start.

I don't think God is going to duplicate exactly what has happened here in Modesto, but He can certainly make this kind of thing happen in other cities. If I were from another city and wanted to begin a similar movement of unity, I would bring together four or five pastors from this group here with four or five pastors from that city for four days of prayer, asking God to give us a starting place.

D. OBSERVATIONS:

1. The size of the church and the status of the pastor should not determine the circle of friends or relationships he pursues.

2. A church should not encourage people to attend churches along economical or racial lines. As a united church, Modesto is attempting to erase social, racial and economic lines. Pastor Darius Crosby's desire is that believers attend anywhere they want and worship as one body of believers.

3. An event such as Meeting At The Tracks is a useful and necessary step in race reconciliation as well as community church unity.

4. Humility is a prerequisite for racial unity to occur.

5.   The Prayer Summits were the place where racial rec-
     onciliation really took hold in Charlie Crane's heart. A
     Prayer Summit with a few pastors from Modesto join-
     ing a few pastors from a community desiring a move-
     ment of unity would be a good starting place for that
     community.

6.   For a ministerium to succeed at racial reconciliation,
     it's leadership must be an ethnic mix. Meetings must
     not always be on "white turf."

Chapter 12

The Church of Modesto City-Wide Rally

A. INTRODUCTION

A HIGH SCHOOL stadium filled with a cheering crowd isn't an unusual sight, especially during football season. But what happened Sunday night in Modesto was, well, downright Heavenly. That 7,000 people braved the mid-90's heat to gather at Johansen High School was a bit amazing in itself. But the Christian community's *"Break Down the Walls"* rally was notable for a much more important reason. It was designed to tear down the barriers that have divided and separated area churches for so long.

• It brought together people from throughout the area, from Modesto and Merced, Tuolumne and Turlock, Escalon and Empire, and most of the communities in between.

• It brought together people from varied denominations, Baptists and Brethren, Pentecostals and Presbyterians, Methodists and Assemblies of God, and the many in between.

• It brought together people from big churches, small churches, rich churches, poor churches, black churches, Hispanic churches, Spanish-speaking churches, and Cambodian-speaking churches, and others in between.

It was a truly ecumenical moment for this region which boasts a world of religious and ethnic diversity. "God is tearing down the walls people have worked so long to build up," worship leader Kevin Friesen told the enthusiastic crowd. "In the big throng of people we're all different. Some of us may not know each other, some of us may not like each other, but we are all brothers and sisters tonight."

Modesto Bee, July 10, 1996

B.   INTERVIEW WITH CLIFF TRAUB, [27]
PASTOR OF BETHEL CHURCH

Cliff is the Executive Presbyter for the Assemblies of God Denomination, as well as serving as Pastor of Bethel Church in Modesto. He served as the coordinator of both the 1995 and 1996 Church of Modesto stadium rallies. Pastor Traub has a deep love for the Lord. He is a man of great administrative abilities and a heart for church unity.

Q.   Cliff, would you please give a little of your background and how you are related to the Church of Modesto?

A.   I serve as Executive Presbyter of the Assemblies of God for Region Four. I oversee ninety churches and 250+ ministers. In our government structure what that means is that each church has its own pastor. Those pastors have a Presbyter over them who is a pastor as well. Then the Executive Presbyter is over all of it. I meet with ten leaders of our district. We serve as the Executive Presbyter of the Northern California/Nevada district, and there are 460+ churches in that. We meet, handle business and ministerial relations problems. I hold business meetings in churches where there is a problem. The Presbyter handles a lot of things. When there is a major problem, they call me in. Every Assembly of God member has a right to talk to me. In our structure it would be almost like a bishop. I pastor at Bethel Church in Modesto as well as serve as an Executive Presbyter.

Bethel Church was one of the oldest. It started in 1917 and became an Assemblies of God Church in 1924. From 1924 to 1985 it was located on Fifteenth and G Streets, then moved to Scenic Avenue. I have served here for sixteen years as Pastor. Almost all of the Assembly of God churches in the area, nine in Modesto, twenty three within a fifteen-mile radius of Modesto, and thirty eight churches in the section between Patterson and Turlock, started out of Bethel or one of our daughter churches.

The Assemblies movement began in Hotsprings, Arkansas, in 1914. Our headquarters is in Springfield, Missouri. There are probably six million people in the United States, and thirty million overseas. We are doubling every five years. In the local church, missions is one of the main themes.

Q. Cliff, where did you come from, go to school, what brought you to Modesto?

A. I went to college in Eugene, Oregon and then pastored a pioneer church outside of Eugene, called Goshen Assembly of God, for sixteen years from 1967 to 1982. That church grew to 1,200. The thing we enjoyed there were the forty adults that came out of that church and are now in full-time ministry. Then I came here. So in thirty two years of ministry I have served in two places.

Q. You served as the Coordinator of two city-wide rallies in 1996 and 1997. How did your ministry contribute to the great sense of unity that the Church of Modesto is experiencing today?

A. In 1996 what we had originally planned was an Assembly of God rally. Because of what God was doing with the Prayer Summit, the Wednesday prayer times, the Meeting At The Tracks, and the National Day of Prayer, I felt it would be too exclusive. God was reaching out. I took it to the Steering Committee

Reverend Cliff Traub — Pastor of Bethel Church — Stadium Event Coordinator.

even though I am not on it. The only condition I asked was if the Steering Committee wanted to take it over and make it a Church of Modesto thing, just keep our speaker, because it was the General Superintendent of our Assemblies, Dr. Tom Trask. They did that. The miracle of it was how little time we had to put it together. We made some initial contacts, but we got the stadium, the staging, the lighting and sound. These are enormous things to get. If I remember right, Kevin Friesen from First Baptist Church was my right arm. We set it up with three different committees. We had the Stadium Committee, the Promotions Committee which handled budget, and the Program Committee. Kevin handled the Program, Glen Berteau the Promotions, and Scott Ousdahl oversaw the Stadium. The miracle was that in three months everything came together. We did it on the July Fourth weekend, following the Promise Keepers Rally in Oakland. There was a momentum coming off of that weekend. We were looking at about 4,000 to attend. In reality, nearly 8,000 participated. We had never done anything like that other than when Luis Palau came in 1983. It was an awesome thing.

One of the points to remember included taking an offering for the burned-out churches in the South. The offering that night was $28,000. Another point was that the event was able to occur because the churches had given toward the budget of $15,000.00. I will never forget the support and applause of the people when the ministers came to the front of the stadium that night.

Q. How did the Stadium Celebration contribute to the great sense of unity that the Church of Modesto is experiencing?

A. When the lay members of our congregation, who are together in the work place, saw the pastors and leaders walking together and the choir with different ethnic groups and denominations, it made a great impression. It was even written up in the Modesto Bee with an "AMEN" at the end of it. Teen Challenge and a minister to recovering addicts were involved in the clean up. They had it cleaned in no time at all. The Youth for Christ teams manned the refreshment booths. Different churches took different responsibilities. There was a real sense of involvement from many groups to make it happen. All of us submitted to the Steering Committee.

The name of the evening was called *"Break Down the Walls."* The second stadium event was called *"We Have a Dream"* and was held on September 14, 1997. The speaker was Tony Evans. We added the Spanish translation by providing headsets in Spanish.

Q.   Had God done anything in your heart to prepare you personally for this movement of unity?

A.   Never before had I worked with so many different denominations and felt like a team player. I never got trapped in denominationalism. The *Meeting At The Tracks* was a real moment of truth for me. My wife and I host a Wednesday television program called *The Eleventh Hour.* It is a daily television ministry that's been here for twenty years. For four years we have been a regular host. In doing that we would bring out guest speakers. Friendships and relationships really grew out of that and we saw the need for getting other churches involved. But at the *Meeting At The Tracks,* when we got ready to cut the ribbon the train came and separated us, it was a visual for me. We have allowed too many things to separate us. I felt that was something profound.

There was also something that happened in the Pentecostal circles in Memphis, Tennessee, about that time.

We called it the Memphis Tennessee Miracle. What happened was the African-American Church of God in Christ is the largest Pentecostal denomination. The white and African-American element came together at that meeting. The white washed the feet of the black, the black washed the feet of the white. It was an incredible thing. It occurred in 1996 and involved 1,000 people or so. The separate organizations were dissolved that day, and a new multi-ethnic fellowship was formed. To see this, and the Meeting At The Track, I thought, "This is what God is doing." I have always operated under the premise, "It is not a matter of getting God to bless what I am doing, it is to find out what God is blessing and then do it."

Praying with other pastors is key for me. I have them on my calendar: the first week in January and every Wednesday I am in town. To tell you honestly, sometimes it is a sacrifice, but it is something we dare not let go of.

Q.   Were there any bench mark events or statistics with the stadium?

A.   The first year there were 8,000 participants. The second year was closer to 10,000. The second year we waited until after football season so we could be on the football field. We had several thousand chairs in the field. That night we had terrible weather, unusual for this area. The winds were swirling, there was talk of tornados thirty miles north of us in Stockton, but the Lord certainly had His hand on the weather that night. You could almost see the hole in the weather pattern above the stadium. There was a cross set in the center of the field. The focal point was not the speaker, Tony Evans, or the music, but the cross. We all turned from

Stadium Event "We Have a Dream" where nearly 10,000 Modesto Christians worshipped shoulder to shoulder.

the stadium, back side, front side, every direction and faced the cross, singing. It was an incredible rallying point. A sense of God's Spirit.

I dare not overlook the Saturday evening before the event! We had a prayer meeting at the stadium. It was awesome to see different members of different churches prayer-walking every bleacher, the field and the track. We must not forget that night of prayer.

Q. Why do you think God chose Modesto to begin such a work in our city?

A. Look at the name Modesto, which means, "modest" [in Spanish]. I don't think that is a small item. When I go to different towns, the most frequent comment I hear is, "We can't get the big churches to cooperate." Here large and small size churches work together and pray together. The pastor of a small church is just as important to the ministerium as the staff of large churches. I think we have some terrific pastors in this town, but they recognize it is God who is moving in Modesto, not their own egos and brilliance. I have thought, "Isn't it wonderful. Modesto has always been known as the home of Gallo Wine Company. Now it is becoming known as the Church of Modesto as well."

Q. Do you see any downside to the unity of the Church of Modesto?

A. I wish we felt we covered the bases with some of the ethnic groups that do not feel we care about them. That is a downside we need to do something about. I am involved in the Martin Luther King March next year. I didn't think I was prejudiced to the point of doing any harm to my ethnic brothers. On the other hand, I don't know that I was doing anything to support them either. I have apologized to them on television and in person, but apologies are easy. What can I do tangibly?

I have discovered in our employees manual that we had seven or eight paid holidays, but Martin Luther King's birthday was not one of them. I went to the Board and said we need to do something. From now on that will be a paid holiday. Someone said, "That's not a big thing." Well, a lot of things are not big deals, but it's a matter of doing the right thing. We are doing that because we want to do what is right.

The downside is that we won't cover all the bases no matter how hard we try. Somebody may feel left out. But I know what our heart is. We are also not concerned with breaking down too much and becoming a homogeneous church because our emphasis has not been to change our distinctives, but to focus on our commonalities. We want to win a city and together we are much stronger than separate.

Q.   What lessons or principles have you observed here in Modesto which could help other communities bring their churches together?

A.   The first thing is they have got to "want it." They must have a deep desire for it. I know that sounds so simple, but I have spoken to several ministerial groups and I hear the same things. They are "too busy," they have "too much on their agenda," they don't know "how the pentecostal and conservatives will get along," or "how will this and how will that . . . ."

Now this may have been an issue for a few men here, but on the whole that was not a problem. Guys don't see me as Assembly of God now. They see me as Cliff. The first thing is, how badly do you want God's blessing on your city? I am not talking about compromised doctrine or changing to become this or that, but how badly do I want to link up with someone who believes in the Bible, in salvation, in the second coming of our Lord, and in prayer?

The principle that goes along with that is a praying attitude. If you pray with someone for a while, it is hard for you to criticize that person. You start carrying their burdens. You must begin to pray over each other, pray blessings on each other. We are not in a competition.

We are a team. Pastors must begin to feel the freedom to get together and be real.

A third area was the Community Marriage Covenant. I think that the covenant set a stage for cooperation. I think this opened a door that helped us. It set a precedent.
We are called to a city and not to a church. The more I think about that call, the more I feel responsible to pray blessings over other churches.

C. OBSERVATIONS

1. A community must possess a "want it" attitude in order to be successful at developing citywide church unity.

2. Praying together, and for one another, must be developed as a foundation for unity. Prayer was the motivation behind the stadium event — as well as a major part of the program.

3. As communities, churches need to develop cooperative policies and stand together with them. Some examples are the Community Marriage Policy and church discipline.

4. Pastors need to possess a sense of calling to a city, not simply to a church. In order for the commitment to the other churches and pastors to grow, a commitment to the city must be made first.

Chapter 13

THE COMMUNITY MARRIAGE POLICY

A. INTRODUCTION

I WAS PROMPTED to do something unprecedented when asked by the *Modesto Bee* to speak to the clergy of Modesto, in Central California, in September 1985. As the paper executives looked on, I began with a prayer: 'Lord, You know that I have failed every time I have tried to create a Community Marriage Policy in other cities. I ask You to give me Your words that would move the hearts of those here. And I ask for ears to hear what You would want these pastors to do to cut the divorce rate in Modesto.' From the corner of my eye I could see my editor and publisher squirming and turning red. But I plunged ahead, trusting the Lord:

Marriage-saving answers can be seen in Catholic, Evangelical, and mainline churches. But they are not learning from each other. Stretching out engagements increases the odds that couples will make mature choices. If Catholics are requiring six months of marriage preparation, can Protestants agree to four months? Catholics are training lay couples as mentors and routinely administer a premarital inventory to help the couple measure compatibility. Don't those steps make sense for your churches too? ...What I want you to consider is an agreement, a covenant that stretches across denominational lines, so that it means more to get married in any Modesto church than it does before a Justice of the Peace.[28]

Before a speech to the Modesto Ministerium in 1985, Mike McManus began with a prayer. This was something he had not done before. "Please give me either the words, or the ears that could make a difference," he prayed. Then he gave his usual speech. That day in his audience were ears that made a difference.

Jim Talley, then Singles Pastor of First Baptist Church, was there. His experience with single adults led him to write *Too Close, Too Soon,* his book on short romances. With Talley as it's coordinator, the nation's first Community Marriage Policy went into effect in Modesto in January,1986. It was signed by one Rabbi and ninety five priests and pastors from nineteen denominations.

In 1986, Stanislaus County had 1,923 divorces. This was a divorce rate of 6.3 per thousand. In 1995, the same area had only 1,606 divorces. Considering that the county experienced an almost 39 percent population increase during those years, the figure is extremely significant. If divorces had increased in proportion with the population, there would have been 2,672 of them. As it was, Modesto had 1,066 fewer divorces than expected for an actual divorce rate of 3.8 per thousand. A decrease of almost 40 percent![29]

The following chapter includes The Greater Modesto Community Marriage Policy and interviews with both Dr. Jim Talley and Michael McManus. Their work on the Community Marriage Policy has not only impacted marriages in the Modesto area, but it made one of the first and most significant contributions to a sense of partnership or team unity within the Modesto Ministerium.

B. THE GREATER MODESTO
COMMUNITY MARRIAGE POLICY

I. Marriage is holy

One concern as ministers of the Greater Modesto Ministerial Association is to foster lasting marital unions under God, and to establish successful spiritual families. Most marriages are performed by pastors, and we are troubled by the extremely high divorce rate nationwide. Our commitment is to help radically reduce the divorce rate in our churches.

It is the responsibility of pastors to set minimal requirements to raise the quality of commitment in those we marry. We believe that couples who seriously participate in premarital testing and counseling will have a better understanding of what the marriage commitment involves. As servants of God, acting on His behalf, we feel it is our responsibility to encourage couples to set aside time for marriage preparation, in addition to concentrating on wedding plans. We acknowledge that a wedding is but a day; a marriage is for a lifetime.

II. Scripture:

"What God hath joined together, let no man put asunder" (Matthew 19:6); Malachi 2:13-16; Ephesians 5.

God has established and sanctified marriage for the welfare and happiness of the human family. For this reason our Savior has declared that a man shall leave his father and mother and be joined to his wife, and the two shall become one. By His apostles, He has instructed those who enter into this relation to cherish a mutual esteem and love; to share in each other's infirmities and weaknesses; to comfort each other in sickness, trouble, and sorrow; to provide for each other and for their household; to pray with and encourage each other, to live together as heirs of the grace of life; and to raise children, if there are any, in the knowledge and love of the Lord. We believe, therefore, that divorce was never an option in God's plan for marriage, and is in fact contrary to His plan. Divorce became an unfortunate consequence of the failure of men and women to fully embrace and enjoy marriage as instituted by God.

III. Implementation: These are the minimum expectations.

A. Waiting Period: A minimum of four months from the initial marital appointment until the wedding date.

B. Premarital Counseling: Minimum of two sessions that would include a relational instrument, inventory or test to help the couple evaluate the maturity of their relationship objectively; recommend that the couple complete a premarital course, which should cover the following critical issues in marriage: God's plan for marriage, communication and conflict resolutions skills, financial management and household budgeting, intimacy in marriage.

We further encourage churches to develop or utilize resources for singles that address issues relating to dating, selecting a spouse, and friendship, which would help prepare them for the premarital process.

In circumstances involving blended families (step

families), special premarital preparation is recommended in the form of workshops, seminars or counseling to address the unique challenges of blending families following deaths of spouses or divorce.

C. Postmarital: We commit ourselves to help troubled marriages, and enrich new marriages.

1. Troubled Marriages. For troubled marriages, we recommend providing referrals to existing Biblically based ministries, seminars, or professional counselors depending upon the need, and develop ministries or seminars dedicated to reconciling the marital relationship. Such resources might include a local Reconcilers ministry, Marriage Encounter, Retrouvaille Marriage Ministries International, Association for Couples in Marriage Enrichment, and/or Dove Christian Fellowship. It is recommended that current ministry/seminar resources and schedules be kept at church offices for ready referrals.

2. Professional Counselors. We recommend that professional counselors be interviewed by the local church to ensure doctrinal integrity, personal membership in a church, church involvement (such as small groups, home/cell church, specific ministries), and philosophy on long vs. short term counseling.

3. Newly marrieds. We recommend attendance at a marriage enrichment seminar (such as Marriage Encounter) within the first two years of marriage, and mentoring by equipped, spiritually mature couples.

D. Scriptural References: Teach Biblical doctrines on morality, marriage, and divorce. Encourage couples to memorize key verses on marriage. Scriptural references may include: Genesis 1 and 2; Deuteronomy 24; Proverbs, Malachi 2, Matthew 5, Matthew 19, Mark 10, Luke 16, I Corinthians 6 and 7, Ephesians 5, Colossians 3, Hebrews 5 and 13, and I Peter 3.

IV Optional Helps: We encourage churches to develop or partner with other churches or organizations that have the resources to offer the following marriage ministries:

A. Engagement Seminar: Encourage couples to participate in a concentrated period of joint introspection, and provide resource lists of recommended engagement seminars.

B. Mentor Couples: Seek to provide as needed a mature married couple to meet with premarital or newly married couples to provide Biblically-based mentoring and accountability. For newly married couples, we recommend that "mentor couples" meet with them at least four times during their first year of marriage. Churches are encouraged to provide or network with other churches to obtain training and refresher training for mentor couples.

V. Pastor's Covenant:

In order to substantially reduce the divorce rate in our area, and to promote God's plan for marriage, I covenant to:

A. Build successful spiritual families;

B. Follow scripture and to implement these minimum preparations for the couples that I marry;

C. Join with other spiritual leaders to encourage couples to seriously participate in premarital preparation;

D. Teach and counsel singles and young people that sexual intimacy is a God-given blessing for a married man and woman only, and that sexual intimacy outside of marriage is a sin according to the Bible;

E. Teach and counsel that reconciliation with God and spouse should be the first priority of either party in a troubled marriage relationship. "All this is from God, who reconciled us to himself through Christ and gave us the ministry of reconciliation" (2 Corinthians 5:18).

_____   _____

Signature   Date

C. INTERVIEW WITH DR. JIM TALLEY [30]

Dr. Jim Talley was one of the original authors of the Community Marriage Policy. He is author of *Too close, Too Soon,* and *Reconcilable Differences.* Both are practical books in the area of Christian relationships and marriage preparation. He served as Minister to Single Adults at First Baptist Church of Modesto for over fifteen years. He is currently working as an independent relationship and marriage counselor and conference speaker. He lives in Oklahoma City with his wife, Joyce.

— Courtesy of Jim Talley

Dr. Jim Talley, Former Minister to Single Adults at First Baptist Church of Modesto and one of the original authors of the Community Marriage Policy.

Q. Dr. Talley, would you please give a little background on how you are related to the Church of Modesto?

A. I came to Modesto in the fall of 1967. I visited the First Baptist Church before Pastor Yeager came. It was not a healthy place to be. I joined another church for five years and worked in a street ministry during that time called the Church in the Park. It was a street ministry which ten churches were supporting, but only First Baptist Church would allow the hippies to come in their services. In fact Pastor Yeager moved the front pews out of the church and let the kids come sit on the floor and be a part of that. I finally went to First Baptist Church because my church wouldn't allow the kids to be a part of the ministry there.

In 1971 I left the Church in the Park and entered the intern program at First Baptist. I started going to the seminary and working with the single adults.

It was the following year that several of us were ordained. I was ordained with Loyal Freisen, Bill Stewart, about five of us. We were all lay people at the time. We had all come up through the ministry, that was one of the unique things we were doing at the time. The church opened the doors and allowed lay people to come into the ministry from the professional world.

We were already involved in working with the single adults. I had been working with hippies on the streets since 1970. At it's peak in 1969 and '70, we were running 300 to 400 kids, and by '74 or '75 there were five facilities sleeping fifty to sixty people a night. We put 5,000 young men through one of our live-in houses, called the Way House, in a twelve-month period of time. I had lots of exposure to young people dating, and people who were messed up in their relationships. As a result I started doing the relationship instruction and brought it into the church.

In about 1970, I formalized the teaching as a seminar on dating relationships. Then I actually came on the church staff part-time in '72, and then full time in '74. As I worked with singles, I was running into all these divorced people. I expanded the material to include divorce and remarriage. In 1985 the new religion editor, Judy Sly, brought Michael McManus in to speak because he was a columnist in the paper. It was a secular promotional thing for the newspaper. They invited all the pastors to come down to the *Bee* office for lunch. That's where Mike presented the concept he had put together that communities ought to make it harder to be married. It was his concept. After that meeting, Pastor Yeager said to me, "Talley, I want you to take hold of that thing and make it work." That was my assignment coming out of that meeting. Pastor Yeager just said, "You will do it."

The meeting was in the summer of '85. Mike returned for the signing in January of '86. There was an update in 1991.

Mike's theory was most of the marriages were taking place in the churches and they weren't working very well. The church ought to grab a hold of it and do something about it.

Q.   How did the Community Marriage Policy contribute to the sense of unity here in Modesto?

A.   I think at that time the Modesto Ministerium was just getting up and on its feet. David Seifert had taken it over. They were pulling and trying to draw the whole community together. We were meeting on a fairly regular basis. What I did with the Community Marriage Policy was go to the Steering Committee for the Modesto Ministerium and ask if this was something they would be willing to get behind and sponsor? They said they would be happy to do that. I said I wanted to put a committee together and start working on that.

We'd bring it back after we got the thing done to see what they thought and see if they would get behind it. The pastor at the Covenant Church, Garth Bollinger, and a lay Catholic woman, (she ought to get more credit for this thing than anybody else) and two others. We met two or three times and drafted up the final copy.

The gal took it around to every Catholic priest in town and got them to commit to it up front. She just beat the bushes. She made the thing work on the Catholic end of it. We brought the thing to the Ministerium and they invited Mike to come and speak. He came. We had it all rigged up so everybody could sign it. He came back to town that second time for the specific purpose of presenting it. That, I think, was the first real project the Ministerium got behind, which actually picked up the momentum of the whole community. There were about ninety six guys who signed that original document from about thirty seven or forty different churches.

I think once it passed through the Ministerium and they got behind it, we did a whole lot of stuff in the local area. We presented it in Turlock, Tracy and several areas around us, getting the people behind us. That really pulled the whole community together with a sense of camaraderie and developed the Mo-Town, the early Mo-Town concept.

From there the thing just took up a life of its own. Mike took what we did. As he continued to go and speak and talk around the country, he used that example of what we'd actually done. He began to get other communities to do it.

Q. Why do you think God chose to do something like this in Modesto? Of all cities, why here in Modesto?

A.   I've always felt like God just drew some people to that place. I think He just put His finger down on the ground and said, "I'm going to do a great thing on this geography." Then He brought some people to that place. I think God brought Pastor Yeager there. I think He brought Pastor Seifert there. I think He brought the key players to that place. I think it was more the people that He got to come there than what was going on there. I've always felt God just picked a spot on the ground geographically and then drew some key people there. I think it was just a commitment of the people and the environment that was there, and the spiritual growth. God just did some unbelievable things in that city. I think it started at Orangeburg Baptist Church, moved to First Baptist Church, has continued to spread to Calvary Temple, then Big Valley Grace Community Church, and now many others. I think it has impacted every church in that town. It was a real turnaround in the whole city. I think it was just the grace of God to pick a spot and to bring people there. He found people who were willing to give 110% of their lives.

Q.   Do you see any objections or a downside to this kind of unity?

A.   I think the only thing we ran into of a downside is it put a lot of pastors in a position of having to say no to their Board or leadership. For instance, after you sign the Marriage Policy, what do you do when the Chairman of the Board of Deacons comes and says, "My kid's got this girl pregnant and I want you to marry them next Saturday at my house." I think that would put a lot of people in real distress. Also, some of them felt like they got in trouble with their denomination, which held their retirement fund, and the denomination wants to edict those kinds of things. I would say that the downside is probably less than 1%.

Q.   What lessons or principles have you observed here in Modesto that are transferable to other communities?

A.   I think the willingness to sign a common document, that was broad enough anybody in town could sign it, brought a real sense of unity. We saw that in Turlock, and in Tracy. I've seen it all over the country where I travel and speak. Any lay person in town can take that document and go to his pastor or the ministerium. I think it would draw the whole community together.

[*See appendix for contact information for Dr. Talley*]

C.   INTERVIEW WITH MICHAEL McMANUS [31]

Michael McManus is a syndicated newspaper columnist writing on issues of Ethics and Religion, a radio commentator on family-related news, and former TIME magazine correspondent. He and his wife, Harriet, live in Bethesda, Maryland. The following interview was done by phone, August 12, 1998.

Q.   Michael, would you give a little of your background and how you're related to the church of Modesto.

A.   I'm a nationally syndicated columnist. I've been writ-
      ing a column called "Ethics and Religion" since 1981.
      One of the newspapers that published my column for
      more than a decade was the *Modesto Bee*. In my
      research, in my work in writing this column, I had a
      particular interest in writing about how some churches
      were doing a better job in strengthening or saving mar-
      riages. I wrote a number of columns along this line,
      but I could see no affect of the columns. It was sort
      of like dropping a cup of water into the ocean. It still
      looked the same. I began to be invited by newspa-
      pers or clergy groups to speak to them because the
      column was published locally. Sometimes the editors
      would like to bring in the guy who's writing every week
      so the people can see who this is and ask him ques-
      tions, or criticize or him, or whatever they wanted to
      do. I began in 1984 suggesting to clergy they consider
      creating what I called a Community Marriage Policy,
      whose goal would be to consciously push down the
      divorce rate of the community. I noted that in Europe,
      where only 10% of the people go to church on Sunday,
      their divorce rate is about half that of the United States;
      countries like France, Germany where only 10% of
      the people are going to church on Sunday. We have
      40% of the people in church on Sunday in this country.
      Our divorce rate should be below that of Europe, not
      above it. Not twice as high if the church were doing
      its job.

      The problem in part is most churches are blessing ma-
      chines, or wedding factories, when it comes to mar-
      riage. They grind out those weddings on Saturday
      without an awful lot of follow up of whether they're
      going to work or not. There's no plan to strengthen ex-
      isting marriages in the average congregation. There's

no plan to save the troubled ones, except to refer them to counselors who are usually ineffectual. Marriage is a very low priority in most churches. I said it should be a high priority, the heart of the problems of America, the most domestic problems of America. Most people would point to, for example, promiscuity, high abortion rates, illegitimacy rates, high divorce rates; all these things come down to the fact that the family structure is collapsing. The church has a particular responsibility to hold marriages together. What God has joined together the church should hold together, I argued. In most cases the churches are not doing much. Not because they don't want to, but because they don't know what works.

As a journalist I deal with this in my speeches, and I had given this speech a number of times all over the country before it succeeded anywhere. It succeeded in Modesto because of Jim Talley. When I spoke in Modesto, I did something I had never done before. I began with a prayer. I said, "Lord, you know I failed when I've given this speech before in other places. Please give me either the words, or the ears that could make a difference." As I was saying this, I looked out of the corner of my eye. I could see my editor and publisher from the *Modesto Bee,* Sanders LaMont, was sitting there squirming because I was embarrassing him. What did happen that day was Jim Talley. It did sink in on him. He did something that you think would have occurred to me as a writer, to write down the specifics of what I was proposing on a single page.

The *Modesto Bee* paid my way to come that first time. Jim raised the money from local churches for me to come back and speak. I spoke on a Sunday night to one of the churches. On Monday we met with the clergy a second time, in January of 1986. It happened to be the day of the Challenger disaster. It was one of those days where fog is thicker than soup. Driving down from San Francisco I could hardly see my hand in front of my face. I heard about the disaster as I was driving in. When I spoke the second time, I quoted scriptures for the first time on certain things. I said, "Paul said the job of the pastor is to equip the saints for ministry or train God's people for service. What more important ministry or service is there than saving marriages. Who's better qualified to do this than couples with good marriages that you can find in any church." I made another point in the second time I spoke that directly related to this question of unity. I said, "Jesus in His High Priestly prayer, reported in Chapter 17 of John, prayed that His followers would be one as He and the Father are One, so that they, the unbelievers, may believe that You sent Me. If Modesto were to adopt a Community Marriage Policy and be the first city in the country to do it, you would be a city on a hill, to use another phrase of Jesus.

Q.   How do you think the Community Marriage Policy contributed to the great sense of unity in Modesto?

A.   What I'm saying here is that if the churches perceive themselves as a city on a hill, and at least on the question of marriage there was unity, churches are going to disagree on questions like abortion and other things. They ought to at least be able to come to consensus on the issue of marriage. We all want to strengthen all the marriages in our churches, save the troubled ones, and equip those who are preparing for marriage, for a life-long marriage. We should be able to agree on these minimums and take what has worked in some denominations, or some churches, and plant them in all the churches in the community. Things like a minimum time of preparation, a premarital inventory, the training of older couples with solid marriages to mentor the younger couples, and the encouraging of all existing marriages to have their marriages refreshed.

You have done some of those things and your community is stronger for it. In fact Modesto has received some national press for the community marriage policy. Peter Jennings has a story on the ABC World News Tonight, Tom Brokaw did a story on NBC Nightly News, and George Lewis, the correspondent for NBC on the west coast, came up to Modesto. Dan Rather introduces a 48-Hour segment in which they talk about Modesto. And there was the Los Angeles front page story that took a look at this.

Modesto has come together and has also become *"a city upon a hill."*

Q.   Were there any bench mark events or statistics with the Community Marriage Policy we should be aware of?

A.   Sure.   The divorce rate now, at least from 1986 to '96, shows the divorce rate is down 35%. No city has had such a large drop in its divorce rate. That's evidence that the Holy Spirit is working there and that marriages are being saved. A 35% drop in the divorce rate. Had the divorces remained level with the population growth, the population of Modesto has grown–well, let me give you the actual numbers so you can have them on hand because it's a little complicated. Between 1986 and 1996 the County's population grew from 303,000 to 420,000. That's a 38.6% jump in the population.

The number of divorces fell from 1,923 in 1986 to only 1,606 in 1995. In 1996 the number was a bit higher than that, I don't have it in front of me now. Had the Modesto area's divorces simply grown with the population, there would have been 2,672 divorces in 1995, not 1,606. Modesto, or Stanislaus County to be more accurate, is now saving more than 1,000 marriages a year.

The national numbers: in 1986 there were 1,178,000 divorces, and in 1996 it was 1,159,000. That's only a drop of 1.6%. The Stanislaus County drop of 1,000 is a very large percentage of the nation's drop.

I have used Modesto in my speeches all over this country. I have helped organize, and I have personally been involved, on the refining of the Community Marriage Policy in seventy of the ninety one cities that now have one. I in effect am citing this *city on a hill* as an example and encouragement to Columbus or Auclaire, Wisconsin, to Montgomery, Alabama, where I was most recently saying if Modesto can do it, you can do it. I called attention to it in my book. Now these numbers here are more dramatic after I wrote the book than they were when I wrote the book in 1993.

Q.   Why do you think God chose to begin such a work in our city? You talked about Modesto being a light on a hill.

A.   First of all, the Lord works through people. He was working through Jim Talley at that time. He was moved and he was able to persuade his senior pastor to get involved. I give Jim Talley credit for listening to the Lord in this and stepping out in faith to try to make something happen. He brought me back a second time. I spoke initially in September, 1995. That is where the *Modesto Bee* was the sponsor. Then Jim drafted a policy and had me come back out in January. Jim helped start some policies in the area, Turlock, Tracy and some other towns nearby. By the time I wrote the book, which was written mainly in 1992, there were only fourteen cities with marriage policies. We now have ninety one. My wife and I have been to thirty seven cities, including Modesto, since January of last year.

I think the fact that I opened with a prayer in my first speech in Modesto may have made a difference. I confessed failure every time I've given the speech, and I'd given it six or seven times up to that point. The fact that Jim was there was important because he had written some books on marriage. I referred to those books in my remarks. The main thing is that people did respond to the call. That response is one the Lord has blessed with these dramatic numbers. If you think about the problem of marriage in America, it is in part a problem of climate. When you and I were young, we grew up believing marriage was for life. Remember? But something happened along the way. Divorces just tripled from 1960 to 1980. Grew from 100,000 to 1.2 million. They have remained at that high level ever since.

We have a million people going to AA [Alcoholics' Anonymous] meetings in this country every week. Every week! Only 10% of the people become alcoholics. But half our marriages are failing. We need to have a cadre of couples who are working with troubled marriages in every congregation. That's one of the things the pastors agreed to do, and I don't know if they've done anything about it. That's part of the new marriage policy, and as far as I know, you've done nothing about it. I'm suggesting how to do something about it here. If you look at page 203 of my book, I give examples of the twelve steps of AA: We admitted we were powerless over alcohol and our lives had become unmanageable. Came to believe that a power greater than ourselves could restore us to sanity. Made a decision to turn our will and our lives over to the care of God as we understood Him.

The movement of God does not respect denominational lines. What I have tried to do in my book and in my work as head of Marriage Savers is to point to whatever works, regardless of where it comes from. I say, look at this. Baptists don't generally look at Episcopal examples. But why not if it works? See, that comes back to the John principle of be one as I and the Father are One.

Charlie Crain asked the toughest question I have been asked in one of these meetings, in which he said, "We have so few people getting married here. I want to jump up and shout 'Hallelujah' when a couple comes in and wants to be married. You're telling me I should have all these hoops to make them jump through. If I tell them they have to go through four months of marriage preparation, take an inventory and be mentored and so on, I'm going to lose them." I said, "Pastor, I don't have an answer for that question," but at the end of the day he signed it. I asked why he had signed it and he said, "Because it was right." When I came back through three years later, he was the first guy I called up. I asked how it was going and he said, "Great man. This is the best thing I ever did. Those couples are now the pillars of my church." I use that story when I talk to black pastors. It's kind of a mini version of what I'm talking about, of Modesto being a city on a hill.

Q. Mike, can you share any lessons or principles which could be transferable to other communities seeking to establish unity in their churches?

A. The churches can cooperate across denominational lines to save marriages. They can do so with programs that work premaritally to help couples avoid a bad marriage before it begins. Of those who take the prepared inventory, 10% break their engagement. Their scores are equal to those who marry and later get divorced. They are avoiding a bad marriage before it begins. That's one of the ways you cut the divorce rate. Second, by giving the inventory and helping the couple address those questions, it helps to strengthen those who do go on and get married. In my church we had 175 couples who went through the program between '92 and '97. Of that number, 25 or 30 broke their engagement or relationship. That's above the national average. But of the 145 or 150 that got married, we only know of three separations now in six years. It's possible to virtually give marriage insurance to the engaged. That's something every church can do across denominational lines.

By having every church train couples in this way, by requiring an inventory, churches are coming together. If they're training mentor couples, they're coming together in that way to do it.

[See appendix for contact information on "Marriage Savers".]

D. OBSERVATIONS

1.   A community marriage policy was one of the first building blocks of unity within the ministerium. It provided a common concern that all pastors could agree on. After prayer, it is a good starting point in moving toward unity. As Mike McManus stated, "Churches can cooperate across denominational lines to save marriages."

2.   There are helps available through "Marriage Savers" for any community to begin a community marriage policy.

3.   Any lay person can start the process of creating a community marriage policy.

4.   A community marriage policy has impacted the divorce rate in Modesto. It can do the same in any community willing to cooperate in a similar way.

5.   In 1985, the year before the first community marriage policy was adopted in Modesto, there were 5.9 divorces per 1000 population. Twelve years later, in 1998, there were 4.1 divorces per 1000 population. Those numbers represented a 30.5% decline in divorce rate adjusting for population increase. During that same period, US divorces dropped from 1,176,000 to 1,163,000 — a decline of only 1.3%.[32]

Year	Population	Divorces	D/1000.[33]
1985	298,400	1741	5.9
1998	427,600	1737	4.1

Chapter 14

Church of Modesto Youth Pastor Network

A. INTRODUCTION

THE YOUTH MINISTERS in a community are often the ones on the cutting edge of ministry. They are usually the pastors who try new and innovative ideas first. In the case of the Church of Modesto, once again they are right there in the front of the pack. They have been working out an effective strategy for reaching the youth of Modesto by linking arms together in ministry for some time. The following interview is with the Director of the Stanislaus County Youth For Christ, Rick Fritzmeyer, who has taken the lead in that attempt. They have named it the Youth Pastors' Network (YPN).

B. CHURCH OF MODESTO YOUTH PASTOR NETWORK MISSION STATEMENT

Philippians 2:1-4

If there be therefore any consolation in Christ, if any comfort of love, if any fellowship of the Spirit, if any affection and mercies, fulfill ye my joy, that ye be likeminded, having the same love, being of one accord, of one mind. Let nothing be done through strife or vain glory; but in lowliness of mind let each esteem others better than themselves. Look not every man on his own things, but every man also on the things of others. (KJV)

Mission:

To exemplify the body of Christ by coming together in love and humility as the Youth Pastors of the Church of Modesto and surrounding communities.

Purpose:

To raise up mature Christian young people who will listen for and follow God's call in their life through prayer and service.

Strategy:

Community: Gathering on a regular basis for prayer and fellowship to encourage one another in our joint ministry of reaching out to youth, strategize together on collaborative events, and uphold one another in Christian love and intercession.

Collaboration:

Events, activities, strategies, and/or campaigns that are created out of a consensus of the group itself. Where the felt need and/or felt strategy wells up from the group and the group as a whole collectively agrees to work together in the facilitation of these various activities. Collaborative events as defined above will therefore hold the unique quality of attaining a 100% participation by the Church of Modesto Youth Pastor Network.

Cooperation:

Events, activities, strategies, and/or campaigns, that are brought to the group by either an outside agency, or predetermined by one of the network members. Originators of cooperative events are welcome to share their activity with the group but must be sensitive to issues of time and scheduling of other members, hence necessitating the need for some to decline participation. Cooperative events may involve as few as two members of the network and still have the network's blessing on such activities, therefore deeming such an activity "A Church of Modesto YPN Cooperative".

Consultation:

As the Youth Pastors of the Church of Modesto we understand many of our congregations do not yet have the opportunity to resource their own youth staff. We acknowledge and proclaim our responsibility and commitment to aid and help these churches as much as possible through:

- providing youth events

- training/mentoring potential youth interns from their local congregation

- providing guest speakers or teachers

- consciously and intentionally thinking of their youth as our own (with regards to the body of the Church of Modesto).

Additional notes:

We hold that collaborative events and the nature whereby they are created is of the highest order of activities we can participate in through the network. Further, because of time and priority issues, we believe that only a few collaborative events a year will be currently possible. Members of the network will covenant to abide by the network consensus and willingly participate in any activities that are deemed a collaborative effort.

Cooperative events, which we also believe have value, will still be encouraged and announced at network meetings, but understandable (due to time constraints and local church responsibilities) will have a lesser priority in the life of the network and it's members. The network strongly encourages those who originate a cooperative event, to be sensitive to these issues and to graciously realize that many may have to decline participation for various reasons. A decline to participate is not a negative or a pulling away,

Youth Pastor's Network: (L to R) *Back row*: Mike Turn, Prescott Evangelical Free; Jeremy McCauley, The Orchard Church; Alonzo Wade, Seed of Joy; Jim Hvisdos, Big Valley Grace. *Middle row*: Rick J. Fritzemeir, Youth for Christ; Eric Chapman, First Four Square; John Liotti, Centro Cristiano Vino Nuevo; (*above*) Chris McPherson, First Baptist Church; Brett Vowell, Orangeburg Baptist; Brad Blakely, Trinity Presbyterian. *Front row*: Tommy McKiernan, Bethel Church; Marty Villa, Youth for Christ.

but rather a simple priority decision that individual members must be allowed to make as they sort through their own vocational calling.

B. INTERVIEW WITH RICK FRITZMEYER, [34] CHAIRMAN OF THE CHURCH OF MODESTO YOUTH PASTOR NETWORK

Rick serves as Executive Director of Stanislaus County Youth For Christ. He is also the Chairman of Modesto's Youth Pastor Network. Rick has a heart for young people and is active working towards the unity within the Church of Modesto.

Q. Rick, would you please give a little of your personal background and how you are related to the Church of Modesto?

A. I have lived in Modesto nine years and served as the Executive Director of Stanislaus County Area Youth for Christ. I grew up in the Placerville area of Northern California, attended Sacramento State College for a couple of years, transferred and graduated from Fresno State for both my Bachelor and Master Degrees. I have served on Campus Crusade for Christ eight years with Athletes in Action. It was on a fund raising trip to Modesto that I became familiar with the area Youth for Christ. We joined the staff in August, 1989. My wife, Marian, and I have been married twenty years and have two high school daughters.

Youth for Christ's primary mission statement is to proclaim the life-changing message of Jesus Christ to every young person. Historically, we are more of an evangelist type organization. As a result of our relationship with the Church of Modesto, we are finding ourselves involved in a multitude of reaching, teaching and building up young people, which frankly we are very excited about. Youth for Christ has been in the area for fifty years. It has had years of tremendous success and some years of quietness. Billy Graham was here in 1948 and was actually on staff with Youth for Christ at the time of that crusade. Although that crusade was not a Youth for Christ sponsored event, Billy Graham was Youth for Christ's first full-time traveling evangelist.

Q.   How has the Youth Pastor Network contributed to the sense of unity in the Church of Modesto?

A.   From the time I arrived in Modesto and before, there have been attempts at a Youth Pastor Network. There were events from time to time that youth pastors partnered on, such as the See You At the Pole, and conferences such as "DCLA", (a Youth for Christ evangelism conference put on every three years.) In some ways the youth pastors have led and in other ways they have trailed behind. There have been different levels and attempts at unity. Some of the rallies, even before my time, have provided a time to come together as youth pastors. Youth Pastors have more fully capitalized on YPN and what that's all about.

Where denominational walls are high ,Youth for Christ can be strong because it can become a safe place for guys and gals to gather. It becomes a neutral territory. In Modesto, because of the unity here, that is not as necessary. However, YFC is still a lead facilitator of the Youth Pastor Network.

Q.   Who were the key people who played a part in the Youth Pastor Network?

A.   One of the main people was Bill Stewart, a long-time youth pastor at First Baptist Church in the 70s and 80s. For many years he ran whatever network existed here in Modesto. He left a stamp of approval for unity between youth pastors. If a network were started today in Modesto, it would not require a Youth for Christ organization to lead it, due to the unity which exists here. However, in another community, Youth for Christ would probably be the logical leader because of its neutrality.

There have been various other Modesto area youth Pastors who have supported the YPN. Currently we do not have a Steering Committee, but for the past year, nearly twenty youth pastors have met on a monthly basis. Different people have taken on leadership roles for different events. However, I continue to be the meeting facilitator.

Q.   Had God done anything in your heart to prepare you personally for this movement?

A.   I was prepared for this and had a heart a long time before it began. I may not have had as big a picture for the potential of the Church of Modesto, but I have always longed for this unity among the Youth Pastors. It is God honoring. Fighting with one another is the extreme. Not fighting is middle ground. Learning to love and embrace each other is where we need to be. The fact we do not have conflict is not where we want to be. We want to go way beyond that. In Modesto I believe we have gone way beyond the arena of conflict.

Q.   Would you share any events or statistics in the Youth Pastor Network that contributed to the Church of Modesto?

A.   Recently Joel Richards, a local Pastor, was looking for a Youth Pastor for the summer. The Junior
High Pastor at Big Valley, David Oats, introduced his
brother, Andrew, who is a youth pastor teacher. Andrew then came and worked in a mentoring capacity
with Cory, the new youth Pastor at La Loma Grace
Brethren. That relationship was a result of the Church
of Modesto and is what the Youth Pastor's Network is
all about.

The first bench mark event was the See You At the
Pole, where students from around the country, over
two million in 1998, got together to pray for their
schools, the teachers and students, and the school
year. This event was student-led, but we did ask Youth
Pastors to attend different schools so that as a Youth
Pastor Network we had an awareness of what was going on citywide. This year we had over 1,000 students
around Modesto campuses.

Four years ago we initiated a praise rally the night before See You at the Pole to encourage the kids and to
give them an awareness of other Christians, both on
their campus and in the other high schools. We met
at Mancini Bowl in Graceada Park. In 1997, 700 students attended. They would come identified with their
church youth group, but would be encouraged to join
their school banner and realize they were not just a
Christian from a particular church. They were also a
Christian from Modesto High or Davis High, because
the next morning that was where they were going to
be.

That event led into our Pray Greater Modesto (PGM)
Crusade. We felt our young people needed to be in
on the ground floor of PGM. We felt their campuses

would be their sphere of influence. The Youth Pastor Network got together and acted rather than being spectators.

Q. Would you share any supernatural experiences when God demonstrated his handiwork in causing the movement?

A. A very significant relational thing happened recently. There was a new pastor in town who had an event in which he had invited all the other churches to participate. I was a little concerned, but I didn't want to discourage him. I knew enough about youth ministry to realize it could create confusion, not because of the Youth Pastor himself, but because of the speaker he was bringing in. Now Youth for Christ is a non- denominational organization and we do our best to remain neutral on doctrinal issues. The speaker, however, was very dogmatic on issues of gifts and doctrinal stands that potentially divide rather than unite. The very thing that the new youth Pastor assured us would not happen, happened. Not because of his fault, but because of the words of the speaker. What was so amazing occurred at the next Youth Pastors Network meeting. In tears, the pastor confessed and asked our forgiveness for misleading us. He had assured us he would maintain control and not let any confusion occur, but of course that happened. There were probably twenty men in the room. By the end of the meeting there was not a dry eye. It was very powerful. Had that not happened, the unity that grew out of those two events would not have occurred. That was probably one of the most supernatural events that occurred. It was tremendous reconciliation and great preparation for what was going to happen.

Q. Why do you think God chose to begin this movement of unity in Modesto?

A. I believe God started to honor the prayers of a few people who prayed that He would unite this community. Some of those prayers go back fifty years. Even back to the Billy Graham Crusade when people prayed God would return His spirit to our town. In the last seven or eight years, the leadership here in Modesto has really actively pursued unity through prayer. "The effective prayer of a righteous man availeth much." Our city is no better, nor no more wicked, than any other city. God has chosen to hear and move on behalf of our prayers for this city.

Q. Is there any downside to the Church of Modesto, the unity being established?

A. No. No, and you know what? Every once in a while when I am tempted to think so, I realize it is because of some personal attitude I have. This attitude, mindset and spirit of love is probably the only real chance we genuinely have to bring reality to the expression, "It is hard to go to hell in Modesto." We have an unusually large number of healthy churches for this size of a city. That in itself was not changing the spiritual climate of Modesto all that much. There are a lot of cities that have many churches per capita in their town, yet these are not impacting their community the way they should. Even if Modesto had twice as many churches, that number would not have the impact individually that the Church of Modesto has collectively.

Q. What lessons or principles have you observed here in Modesto which could help other communities bring their churches together?

A. Human nature has a "cookie cutter" mentality. We try to duplicate what works in other communities. Certainly there are some things which can be transferred to other cities: coming together and learning to pray together. If you took the Harvest Evangelism "Pray Greater Modesto" packet and dropped it on a city whose leaders had not spent considerable time together in prayer, I believe the event would be a failure. Some communities which might try an event only to have it fail could say, "That couldn't have worked there." They may even discount the success of an event in Modesto because of their experience. But the truth is we didn't just start this yesterday. We've been praying together as a ministerium for years. It takes time of prayer and loving one another to lay a foundation for unity.

D. OBSERVATIONS

1. Prayer together is the foundation for all attempts to unite youth pastors from different denominations as well as para-church organizations. It is the groundwork for all other activities. Prayer together must become habitual. The unity movement in Modesto began fifty years ago. It did not happen overnight. It would be unwise for a community of Youth Pastors to meet together in prayer for one month and expect God to suddenly create unity. Certainly God could work a miracle. However, the mindset must be on a long-term commitment to praying together; growing deep as opposed to immediate.

2.   It is essential for the youth workers in a community to cooperate for the sake of the next generation. They must break down walls formed by competitive spirits in order for the next generation to experience the blessings of unity. Absence of conflict is not the goal. Learning to love each other is.

3.   A neutral facilitator, such as Youth For Christ, can be helpful in developing a place for a community's youth workers to cooperate in a non-threatening manner. There is no denominationalism if facilitated by a non-denominational, para-church organization.

4.   There is no formula, package or principle. It is prayer and God's sovereignty which determines the success of an event, program or ministry.

5.   One of the benefits of a Youth Pastor Network is the networking which takes place via the relationships developed. Youth pastors can brainstorm together, serve as resource and accountability partners for each other, and mutually encourage one another in youth ministries. Churches with established ministries can assist churches with new or weaker programs.

6.   Young people on school campuses benefit tremendously from community-wide church unity. Their spiritual survival could depend upon a supportive relationship with a Christian classmate from another church. Young people model what they see. If the community body of believers model unity and consideration for one another, teenagers will have a lesson that is far more influential than any Sunday morning sermon ever could be.

SECTION FIVE

PROJECTS TOGETHER IN SERVICE

"We are one in the Spirit, we are one in the Lord,
We are one in the Spirit, we are one in the Lord,
And we pray that all unity may one day be restored:

We will walk with each other,
                    we will walk hand in hand,
We will walk with each other,
                    we will walk hand in hand,
And together we will spread the news
                    that God is in our land:

We will work with each other,
                    we will work side by side,
We will work with each other,
                    we will work side by side,
And we will guard each one's dignity
                    and save each one's pride:

All praise to the Father, from whom all things come,
And all praise to Christ Jesus, His only Son,
And all praise to the Spirit, who makes us one:

And they'll know we are Christians
                    by our love, by our love,
Yes, they'll know we are Christians by our love." [35]

Peter Scholtes

The greatest work we can do for the Lord is done on our knees, and that has been the emphasis of Modesto's pastors. Prayer and worship are both the preparation and the work which the church is to be about. There comes a time however, when God leads his church to get up off her knees and roll up her sleeves. The following section records the story of two such opportunities. The first is the account of the 1997 Modesto area floods and subsequent work of the Christian community to rebuild the flood victim's homes. The other account is of Modesto's 1996 relief collection for three burned out churches in Mississippi and Tennessee. God was pushing the Church of Modesto toward unity by leading them to work together for the good of His kingdom.

Chapter 15

THE FLOODS OF '97

A. INTRODUCTION

IN DECEMBER 1996, an unprecedented amount of snow fell in the Tuolumne River watershed. In early January a warm rain "pineapple express" storm poured down upon that heavy Central Sierra snowpack, dumping unprecedented amounts of rainfall. The resultant runoff into the Tuolumne River watershed exceeded the capacity of the Don Pedro reservoir, requiring releases which caused water levels to rise above flood stage down stream. Over 5,000 residents were evacuated while approximately 880 homes and businesses were flooded. A complicating factor was the flooding of the Modesto sewer treatment facility which resulted in raw sewage being deposited in homes down stream with devastating results.

While this was occurring, the Modesto Ministerial Association was meeting in the Santa Cruz Mountains for their Third Annual Prayer Summit. Ironically, they were seeking God's direction for the best way to minister to their community. The answer was not long in coming. God's direction was clear! Help in the area of physical relief for the flooded families.

The Ministerial Association moved quickly. Before long they had selected a man to lead the relief project on their behalf. The Greater Modesto Area Churches (GMAC) was established. Chancellor Emeritus Dr. Tom Van Groningen was invited to head up the project.

Tuolumne River flood waters engulfing the Modesto sewage treatment facility and nearby homes.

The following interview is with Tom Van Groningen, retired Chancellor of The Yosemite Community College District. Tom is a man who possesses both superb administrative abilities and a sensitivity to God's Spirit. Both qualities are necessary to head a relief program such as the one upon which The Greater Modesto Ministerial Association was about to embark.

B. INTERVIEW WITH TOM VAN GRONINGEN, [36] DIRECTOR OF GREATER MODESTO AREA CHURCHES (GMAC) FLOOD RELIEF, AND BILL VAN RIET, ASSISTANT

Q. Tom, please give a little of your background and how you are related to the Church of Modesto. Also, give a thumbnail sketch of the flood relief organization which was set up"

A. I'm Tom Van Groningen. I was born and reared in a Christian home. I have maintained that commitment throughout my life. We moved to Modesto in 1974 from Porterville where I had been the Superintendent of Schools. Prior to that I had been a Superintendent of Schools in a small rural area in Fresno County. My area of ministry has been largely in public service. I have always tried to create a positive environment and one that was conducive to the basic values I grew up with and certainly I am committed to today. I have always been active in my church as a Sunday School Superintendent, Teacher, member of the Elder and Deacon Councils. The usual kinds of things that one does in that setting. My ministry has, perhaps, been more by example then it has by direct outreach, in that I have not had experience as a missionary. Nor have I had experience necessarily in working in depth with individuals in a spiritual, one-on-one basis. But I have always tried to live my life as an example that I trust others would emulate.

Q. How did your ministry contribute to the great sense of unity that the Church of Modesto is experiencing today?

Flood waters engulfing the Del Rio mobile home park.

A.   The Greater Modesto Area of Churches (GMAC) ob-
     viously has an interesting history in that it came about
     following the floods of '97. In the weeks immediately
     following the floods there was a significant outpouring,
     an emotional outpouring if you will, on the part of both
     the community at large and the church community.
     As that began to wane when the weather dried and
     the sun came out, the GMMA in particular perceived
     a need for a long-term program. That long-term pro-
     gram they envisioned included the reconstruction of
     homes that had been flooded in this tragic event. Our
     numbers indicate there were in excess of 800 homes
     that had been flooded in the county.

When this was established, our plan was to create this non-profit organization and initially engage the services of a group that was called the "Christian Reformed World Relief Committee." When these folks became available to us, they initially came in and did a needs-assessment of the flooded area. Although we had attempted to make contact with all 800, we did not reach all of the owners. We did make contact with a number of them and in the process identified 130 that we determined were in need of help. These were owner-occupied homes and were individuals who, by way of their own resources, were unable to reconstruct their homes. We, through the GMAC, were able to help them without any strings attached. This was unconditional help!

Q. How did the GMAC contribute to the great sense of unity that the Church of Modesto is experiencing today?

A. I think the Greater Modesto Area Churches (GMAC), having been an outgrowth of the GMMA, contributed to the unity. The support for that concept was very broad-based and resulted in the GMMA churches contributing both their talent and their money. As such it certainly served as yet another layer of glue that bonded this group together and gave them a sense of unity. Although I am not sure that was clearly delineated in the minds of those who initially put this together, it certainly became that.

Q. Who were the key people who played a part in your ministry? What roles do they play?

A. I think the Greater Modesto Area Churches (GMAC), having been an outgrowth of the GMMA, contributed to the unity. The support for that concept was very broad-based and resulted in the GMMA churches contributing Let's begin by looking at the GMMA leadership. Obviously that would include the leaders who served on that Executive Committee. The Executive Committee of the GMMA invited me to have breakfast with them and there laid this on me, and it was just that. They had a general plan of work they had envisioned and needed some help to put this thing together. Peter Johansen was a part of that, and as many in this community know, he is good at twisting an arm here and there to cause certain things happen. I left that meeting without having made a commitment. In the intervening week, I have to say that with all the prayer that was occurring, I was moved to respond affirmatively to this call and get involved in putting this organization together.

In summary, I met with them, we put a Board together, and immediately at their encouragement brought on Bill Van Riet to share the workload. Also Sonja Steens in the office. We then brought on four other people who have worked with us on a limited basis.

The Flood Relief Task Force was composed of Peter Baker, President of Coit Carpet and Drapery; Ross Briles, minister and owner of Fun Works Theme Park; David George, dentist; Lucille Hammer, President, MOCSE Federal Credit Union; Peter Johansen, Retired businessman and minister; Lee Kucker, First Vice President, Smith Barney; Mike Riley, Vice President, Diamond Walnut Growers; and Bob Taylor, Retired School Administrator.

Q.   Had God done anything in your heart to prepare you personally for this movement of unity?

A.   Yes, but I think in perhaps a bit more subtle way. My entire professional career has been one of administering, managing and putting together programs. Suddenly, with this great need having been identified and with GMAC's need for someone to put together and administer the flood relief, my professional experience had groomed me for just such a role. I guess you could say that I sensed the Holy Spirit leading me in this direction.

Q.   Were there any bench mark events or statistics in your area of ministry which contributed to the Church of Modesto?

A.   I think the reference has already been made to the number of homes that have been flooded, the number of assessments that have been made, and then the actual reconstruction that has already taken place on these 130 homes.

As I said before, there were 800 homes that were flooded. There were actually more than 130 that were assessed. More like 200 homes were assessed. Some of those were not owner-occupied and had other resources available. They went ahead on their own. All we did was provide emotional and spiritual support for them. But the 130 were the core-group of individual homeowners who needed help. In setting up this non-profit group, we recognized that the first thing needed to be done was to raise the required capital. We looked to the churches and they were certainly generous in this respect. We also had significant contributions from individuals, and then we were successful in garnering a couple of major contributions from Foundations. Sierra Health Foundation and The California Endowment contributed about $240,000. That,

— GMAC Photo

"The overwhelming majority of our labor was also donated."

added to what we had raised within the community and the national denominational sources, produced about one half a million dollars. If we are looking at bench mark numbers, the actual cash was about a half million dollars. Then we had a substantial amount of in-kind contributions, including the use of a building rent-free and building materials. I am sure that the total of those in-kind contributions exceeded $200,000 to $250,000 in value.

Thankfully it was not necessary to buy all these materials. I might add that the overwhelming majority of our labor was also donated. As I recall, we were averaging about 2,500 to 3,000 hours per house of donated volunteer time. That came from individuals within our community as well as the organizations that I have previously referenced. The Christian Reform Relief Committee in Grand Rapids, Michigan has a pool of 1,500 volunteers. These folks simply make themselves available for three-week cycles. They come from all over the United States and Canada. We provided them a place to live and fed them. In doing so, we were able to accomplish this task. If the labor were to have been purchased, I am sure it would have been in the multi-million dollar range.

Q.   Would you share any supernatural experiences that God demonstrated his handiwork in causing this movement?

A.   My initial experience in that regard was to seek out Bill Van Riet, Assistant Director and Case Manager for the project. Beyond that I have had personal experiences and have had other experiences related to me. Bill and other volunteers have shared stories or their personal contacts with clients which leave no doubt that many lives have been impacted.

Q.   Bill, as Case Manager, would you share a story of how God was involved in this?

A.   We would like to say that we saw "x" number of lives, of people, who were converted to Christianity, but we really cannot say that. I do not know of lives that were completely changed. However, there were many people who have been positively impacted through our efforts. One fellow, Brian Cenesa, had a home in which we did a lot of work. The Christian Reformed World Relief (CRWR) team

Bill Van Riet and Tom Van Groningen of GMAC

did a last-nail ceremony in his home. That was done back in June of '97. We had not heard much from Brian since. At the time he acted rather indifferent to any religious over-tones to that ceremony, but in the meantime we had given him several jobs (he is a vinyl and carpet installer). Some time passed and we called him to install vinyl in another house. He walked in and said: "You know Bill, I haven't been to church in many years. I can't remember the last time I went. But I went last night because I was down and out and broke. So my wife said, 'Come with me to church.' Then you called in the morning for work. I see that as God working in my life!" We do not know what the follow up will be yet, but God knows.

Another example is a gentleman I've been working with for the past two weeks. He lives alone in a home that had been totally devastated. He had some resources, but those were insufficient. Foreclosure procedures had been initiated on the property. We were able to intervene. In intervening, I learned from the private lender that this person had been praying that someone would intervene and stop the foreclosure process. We were apparently the instrument that was used to do that. We have now been able to reconstruct the home in its entirety. The work was all done unconditionally. That is, no strings attached. After observing all the volunteers giving their time for him, the young man now says that Christianity has taken on a totally different meaning. Yes, he did attend church as a youngster, but Christianity has become much more real to him now. His name is Lionel. What will happen to Lionel we do not know, but seeds have been planted, and the Holy Spirit will do His work.

In another incident, our CRWR volunteers were working in a house where it was fairly obvious something was wrong. It was rather apparent to us as they became very discouraged. One particular man, who came from New Jersey, was working in this home and was really questioning what he was doing there. "I don't know if there's prostitution or drugs, or what is going on here, but its not right," he said. That same day when he was asked to go back and finish up the job, a boy came in with a Christian card with a personal note. It read: "You can't know how thankful we are for all of your efforts. We love you. You will have an extra star in your crown when you get there because of what you have done for us." It just melted him, turned him around. His name was Al DeRoo from New Jersey My point is that the blessings were not only received by the clients, but those who worked as well.

These people who came from all over the USA and Canada were Christians, or they wouldn't have been here. For us to see the bonding that occurred among them as they lived together, and the fellowship was a real rewarding experience for us. We have gained tremendously by that. These were unique people who gave up their time and lives for this relief effort.

Q.   Bill, thanks for sharing those stories. Tom, Why do you think God chose to begin such a work of unity in Modesto?

A.   He works in mysterious ways. For me, frankly I haven't been able to put my finger on a reason. It certainly provided an opportunity for the church community to come together. This has gone far beyond the religious community. We have been working with other non-profits, the United Way, the Red Cross, the Salvation Army, the City of Modesto, and the County of Stanislaus. All of these people, including representatives from public and non-profit as well as religious organizations, have worked in a seamless manner as one. The fact is that during the prior twenty years I had worked with these people in different capacities, environments and venues. Suddenly here was an opportunity to bring all of those common experiences into focus on this particular project. If you asked me what God had in mind with the flood, I suspect it was an opportunity to bring this community together and bond. To coalesce its resources and provide a common focus. Maybe even an example to other communities of what can happen.

Q.   What lessons or principles have you observed here in Modesto which could help other communities bring their churches together?

A.   In a broader area than just the religious context, the leadership of the various churches can come together on a regular basis and put aside their denominational differences. They can focus on Christ, that which they have in common and what is really important. In terms of what has happened in this community, I think the flood relief is one additional brick in a foundation which bridges all of the disparities between the churches. It has brought a sensitivity, an acceptance and a tolerance to those involved. One perhaps picks up a different perspective as a participant than as an observer. We've had the opportunity to do both. In addition to the Ministerial Association, I have observed all they have done to bring the religious community together. Now with GMAC, I was able to participate through administrative abilities and reach out to other organizations necessary to bring that coalition into action. I'm not sure that always occurs in a disaster area where there is an interfaith operative, but it did here.

In the final analysis, there were just so many people who were involved in this process. Turf never became an issue. There was one minor incident that surfaced. We just didn't allow it to deter us. We remained focused on the objective. When we remained focused on the objective, the little issues came and went.

C. OBSERVATIONS

1. Natural disasters provide excellent opportunities for a community's churches to rally together and demonstrate Christ's compassion and unity within the Body of Christ. Both to themselves and to a watching world.

2. It is essential by the very nature of disasters that the churches respond quickly to the crisis.

3. In the case of the Modesto Flood of '97, it was a wise decision of the GMMA to hire an outside administrator, Tom Van Groningen, to run the operation. Had any one church directed the work, it would have limited the efforts for obvious reasons.

4. Involving community organizations and government agencies was a wise and effective decision on the part of GMAC. Without the resources provided by these agencies, the total relief project may never have been successfully completed.

5. Involving community organizations and government agencies enabled the church to be "salt and light" to a spectrum of our society which normally has very little interaction with the Christian church.

6. Projects such as the flood relief also provide golden opportunities for Christians to interact with other Christians, across church and denominational boundaries, and enjoy serving together.

7. When the church is unleashed and the Holy Spirit is given opportunity to work in fresh new venues, incredible things can happen.

Chapter 16

BURNED CHURCHES RELIEF PROJECT

A. INTRODUCTION

MEMBERS OF THREE black churches in Mississippi and Tennessee literally shed tears of joy last month when four delegates from the collective Church of Modesto arrived with $30,000.00 to help rebuild their demolished sanctuaries.

"I'd never heard of Modesto before," said the Rev. Perry Carroll, pastor of Central Grove Baptist Church in Corinth, Mississippi. "For them to come down and present a $10,000.00 check — that just totally shocked me. The church is overjoyed."

"It let us know that they were with us and that we all are serving the same and living God, in Modesto and Kossuth, Mississippi," said Charles Dillworth, a Trustee at Mt. Pleasant Missionary Baptist Church.

The Church of Modesto — a name coined by members of the Greater Modesto Ministerial Association to signify the unity of local churches — collected $30,928.00 toward rebuilding black Southern churches destroyed by arsonists. Two pastors — the Rev. Charlie Crane of Greater True Light Baptist Church and the Rev. Jeff Kreiser of Living Faith Community Church — and two laymen–Fred Barry of Victory Life Center and Gordon Headrick of First Baptist Church of Modesto — made the pilgrimage July 27-29, paying their way with their own money and offerings from their churches.

The delegation delivered checks for $10,000.00 apiece to Mt. Pleasant and Central Grove. Another $10,000.00 check went to the Dyersburg (Tennessee) Resurrection Fund to rebuild Mt. Pleasant Missionary Baptist Church in nearby Tigrett.   — *Modesto Bee, August 1, 1996*

B.   INTERVIEW WITH JEFF KREISER, PASTOR [37] OF LIVING FAITH COMMUNITY CHURCH AND PARTICIPANT IN RELIEF TRIP TO MISSISSIPPI

Q.   Jeff, would you please give a little of your background and how you are related to the Church of Modesto?

A.   My wife, Heather, and I came to Modesto on December 22, 1994 from the Los Angeles area. I had attended Fuller Seminary in Pasadena. We came here to start a new church, a work designed as a pioneering church plant sponsored by a dozen churches located from the Bay Area up to Sacramento.

We began services in January of '96. When I moved here there was a pastor named Don Christianson who had been here for about six months or so. He reached out to me and invited me to the minister's Wednesday prayer time He said, "We're praying together as pastors. Come join us." The church he was pastoring at the time was one of our sponsoring churches, the Church of The Cross.

Q.   Would you give us an overview of what happened with the "Burned Churches Relief" and how the Church of Modesto got involved in that?

A.   January of 1996 was the first Prayer Summit I attended and got to know a lot of the pastors. We kind of moved forward and there was the Meeting At The Tracks in March of '96. At that time God was bringing people together across denominational and racial lines in a greater way. The racial aspect of it was really propelled by the Meeting At The Tracks. It created a sensitivity. Now quite a number of the pastors were aware that since the end of '95 and the beginning of '96, there were these church burnings going on in the South. In April after the Meeting At The Tracks, Pastor Dave Seifert of Big Valley brought the burned churches up as a prayer concern during our noon prayer time. It just kind of flowed out of the Meeting At The Tracks and what was happening with the burned churches.

Personally, I just have a burden for racial reconciliation that came out of some work experiences I had while I was in Los Angeles. I was there during the riots. After that prayer time I talked to Pastor David and said "Why don't we flesh this out a little bit." The idea came up for an offering there. At the same time there was kind of the momentum for having the very first Church of Modesto celebration at Johansen Stadium. It was all kind of happening at the same time. I had shared with Pastor Dave about connections I have that would relate to us being able to get money where it was needed most. It was the middle of May. It had been going on for half a year. The media really grabbed the story. That's when there was huge media publicity about churches being burned. The idea of a relief gift was just a timely idea. I suggested that we take it to a church in person. It's one thing to take up a collection and mail a check. It's another thing to give it to a church in person.

I had some connections in the South where we could meet some specific needs. I said, "You can send anybody, it doesn't matter to me, but I'm willing to go. I think that it would be a much more powerful statement to those who are there, as well as to what God's doing here, to do that." What happened in the course of events there was that Pastor Charlie Crane and I were chosen to be the ones who were going to go. We also decided that the offering was too small to just to send us with a few thousand dollars. We would take a collection at the actual stadium celebration event. There was just a huge offering that night. Over $30,000 was received for the burned churches.

Q.   Who were the key people who were instrumental in this project?

A.   I think the whole Steering Committee really had a heart. Pastor Charlie Crane from Greater True Light Church, Fred Barrey from Victory Life Center, Gordon Hedrick, a lay person from First Baptist Church, and me, from Living Faith Church were prayed for, commissioned, and sent. There were two black brothers and two white brothers going to the South. Four men representing four different congregations. All from the Church of Modesto.

Q.   How did this project contribute to the sense of unity in the Church of Modesto today?

A.   An obvious way is simply the makeup of the team which was sent. It couldn't have been much more diverse.

I also think that the unity was mostly in the offering. In the idea that there were people from the Church of Modesto that were taking care of a very practical, physical need. This was kind of a precursor to flood relief effort in January of '97, six months later. It gave an outward focus. I think sometimes a problem with the unity idea is that we end up navel gazing and slapping each other on the back. I think God wants us to love the world and be in the world. Often times, the church is accused, and unfortunately rightly so, of stabbing each other in the back. You know, by not taking care of each other's needs. The whole idea of breaking down the walls in this city is now extending to another part of the nation.

I think it was one of the first things that we broke through to the media, particularly the *Modesto Bee*. It was from that point on that the paper seemed to change concerning the Church and of Christian things. It was exactly one year later that we had a meeting with the staff of the *Modesto Bee*. We heard from them, listened to them and their concerns, as well as prayed over them. There was an incredibly positive editorial concerning the Christian church because here was a hot issue in the public eye. Here was the church responding to a great need with love and grace, as Jesus Christ would. We didn't do it for the publicity, but because it was the right thing to do. But a result of it was that it became recognized.

Talking in the language of today, we met a felt need. We prayed about it, but we also did something about it. It was an answer to prayer. But I think also the fact that everybody at that stadium celebration put in a gift, and the fact was that this wasn't any one church's money. It wasn't Big Valley's money, or Living Faith's money, or Calvary Temple's money, or St. Paul's Episcopal's money. It was God's money given by the Church of Modesto. These were my dollars mingling with everybody else's. Christian. I don't think you can understate the significance of an offering like that. We were literally giving to Jesus through a needy congregation in the south.

Q. Had God done anything in your heart to prepare you personally for this movement of unity?

A.   One thing is that in my background I've had contact with different denominations and different flavors of Christianity. Even though I was raised solidly in one church with a Christian family, I was exposed to many different churches' activities, as well as young life. We visited a lot of different places. We had an openness in my church to want to minister with other churches or, if they had Randy Stonehill over there, we didn't need to bring him here. We'll just go to their Randy Stonehill concert, or whatever. There was a sense of openness and linking in our community.

Then when I went to college there was no church of my denomination there. I was just looking for some really basic things, which were: Jesus Christ is Lord and the Bible is preached. I attended a church of another denomination.

I went to college at Cal Poly, San Luis Obispo. While I was there I was involved in two really breakthrough events. One was simply called Christians Together. It was a precursor to what we're experiencing here in Modesto. An outreach event joining the Navigators, Campus Crusade, Inter- Varsity, a couple of other campus Christian clubs, the Newman Center for the Catholics, and several other different Christian ministries. There was no competitive spirit, just a feeling that, "We need to show this campus that Jesus Christ is what it's about." There were 800 or 900 who came. That happened twice, and I was able to be involved, once from a campus club perspective, once from the church ministry perspective.

One other thing was when I went to Fuller. I worked in northwest Pasadena, which is an African-American area of the city. I was the only white guy, working with an organization that was really seeking to bless and change things for the good.

When I came here and I thought, "This is exactly what needs to happen." The church I worked with down in Los Angeles, had a vision to do something like this, but the barriers were so huge that nothing was really happening.

Q.   Were there any bench mark events or statistics in your area of ministry that contributed to the Church of Modesto?

A.   The significant things about this project were the details: four men from the Church of Modesto hand delivered a total gift of $33,000 to Christian Churches in Mississippi. The gift was given to two churches and a foundation which had been established to assist a third church.

The actual trip dates were July 23 -28, 1996.

Q.   Would you share any supernatural experiences in which God demonstrated His handiwork with the Burned Churches Relief Project?

A.   Oh yes. It's one of those things that I just think was the Holy Spirit. I'm convinced. I think it was supernatural. God's Spirit was giving people a deep conviction that that's the right thing to do. I think the results of it confirms that.

God brought just at the right people together at the right time, Even the right people going on the trip. It was God's timing in that regard. On the trip there were a couple of things in which God showed Himself.

Q.   Jeff, Would you share a story from the trip?

— Greater Modesto Ministerial Association

Church of Modesto representatives Charlie Crane, Gordon Headrick, Fred Barry and Jeff Kreiser.

A. The church services were great in both situations. We went and worshiped with them on a Sunday morning. The foundation was on a Monday, and we brought the money. We went to Memphis, Tennessee, and then we drove to northern, rural Mississippi.

When we landed in Memphis. We were taking the rental-car bus to get our car. There was an older black gentleman driving the bus. He said, "Are you here to party or are you here to eat the barbecue?" We said, "We're here in the name of Jesus Christ. We're here to be black and white together, and we're going to go visit these churches." I'm trying to remember exactly what he said, but he was pretty much in disbelief that we were traveling together and were there for that reason.

In my mind I'm just like okay, just a few miles from here to where black churches were burned to the ground, and here we are at midnight in this diner. Later on a younger black man came in and got an order to go. It was just an interesting experience. So that was one. You can say these were supernatural or you can say it's just God working through people, finally breaking through because we all went to one of the churches. Fred and Gordon stayed at that church to give them their check. Charlie and I went to the other church, which started a little later. Charlie was going to preach there, and did preach there very well. We went into the church. It was very small, twenty five or thirty people. They were meeting in, not a tent but a . . .

When we arrived at Central Grove Baptist Church they asked each of us to share words, and we did. Then an older black gentleman came up to me and shook my hand and said, "You're the first white man who has ever worshipped with us here." Isn't that incredible?

Mt. Pleasant Church had been there since the end of the Civil War, 110 years, and Central Grove had been there for 60 years. Not one white man had ever worshipped there.

Q. Why do you think God chose to begin this movement of unity in Modesto?

A. I think God chose Modesto for two reasons. One, there's nothing–it's a humble city–there's nothing to draw attention to it. There's no great reasons to live in Modesto from the world's eyes. From a world's perspective there's not much view. But from a kingdom perspective God's saying, "I'm going to do something there."

Also, if you look on a map, Modesto's in the very center of California. So goes California, so goes the United States. So goes the United States, so goes the world. If God picks this city that's at the heart of California and can do something, you know it could spread from here. I think it's just the way God would do it.

Q. Can you think of any down side to the unity being developed here in Modesto?

A. No, I don't see anything that could be wrong with unity. It's God's heart for his people.

Q. Do you see any lessons or principles here in Modesto which could help other communities bring their churches together?

A. I would say from my experience, it is necessary to initiate friendships with other pastors of other churches and denominations. If we don't do that, but wait for the other guy to call us, unity will never be achieved.

Maybe another thing, in light of our relief project, is that again we must initiate some form of action towards racial reconciliation. It doesn't necessarily have to be as big as thousands of dollars toward rebuilding a church, but we must start somewhere. The act, no matter how small, will send a clear message of reconciliation to the ethnic churches.

C. OBSERVATIONS

1. The stadium event gave the people of Modesto an opportunity operate as "one church", and for a significant cause as well.

2. Though a small amount of money in terms of the larger national picture, this project was significant for the local churches, both black and white. It provided an opportunity for the COM to do something tangible toward racial reconciliation.

3. It is important to start somewhere in the process of race reconciliation. The key is to start, God will direct the process once a community steps foreward in obedience.

SECTION SIX

CONCLUSION

"We shall be a city upon a hill. The eyes of all people are upon us; so that if we shall deal falsely with our God in this work we have undertaken and so cause Him to withdraw His present help from us, we shall be made a story and a by-word through the world." [38]

John Winthrop

Chapter 17

Concepts

On Citywide Church Unity

"If you read history you will find that the Christians who did most for this present world were just those who thought most of the next. The Apostles themselves ... the English Evangelicals who abolished the Slave Trade, all left their mark on Earth, precisely because their minds were occupied with Heaven. It is since Christians have largely ceased to think of the other world that they have become so ineffective in this. Aim at Heaven and you will get earth 'thrown in'; aim at earth and you will get neither."[39]

C.S. Lewis

CHAPTER 1. INTRODUCTION

BEFORE THE 1980's, the churches in Modesto had much work ahead of them if they were to be termed the Church of Modesto. They were better described as small kingdoms with high walls and very little communication. Their focus was primarily on their own ministries and own needs, with little time to be concerned for other congregations or the city as a whole. This was Modesto's starting point, and yet God has overcome those obstacles. He can do the same in another city with a similar commitment.

SECTION ONE

Past Experiences as Preparation

CHAPTER 2.   THE GMMA – AN EARLY HISTORY

CHAPTER 3.   THE GMMA – A RECENT HISTORY

Modesto's journey down the path of unity initially began in 1948 with the cooperation of churches on the Billy Graham Crusade. It has continued from that beginning with greater intensity in the past 15 years.

Unlike many aspects of modern life, deep rooted unity is not a quick process. A key ingredient to Modesto's unity has been perseverance over many years. The Ministerium has met together for over five years of uninterrupted weekly prayer meetings. At it's inception, none of the Modesto Pastors felt their schedules could afford another weekly meeting, but now most consider this prayer time the high point of their week.

Success requires commitment. A group must make a long-term commitment to pray together to see the long-term benefits of praying together.

God anointed and appointed a leader for His work in Modesto. Dr. Seifert's 15 years of leadership have provided great stability as well as vision of community wide unity, both of which are essential for a deep and lasting unity to be realized. This is not to say a community without strong, charismatic leadership could not achieve unity, only that this was the path down which God has led Modesto.

The Modesto pastors have embraced the same core absolutes. They have stood firm on certain essential Biblical doctrines and extended grace to one another on nonessentials. This attitude has not "watered down" the but has provided a foundation which unity could be built upon.

SECTION TWO

Prayer as The Foundation

The act of praying is what God desires from his churches and shepherds. A community's programs are not what attract His attention, but it's prayers. If we seek to unite our communities, we must first draw near to God together in prayer.

In addition to seeking God's face through prayer, we must watch for His hand as we wait on Him. Once we identify where God is at work, we must follow Him there. He will lead His church to a place where He is already working. For Modesto, it has been in the area of community wide church unity.

It is easy for the "tyranny of the urgent" to crowd out that which is truly important. It will take discipline and a commitment to the process for any community's pastors to set this time aside and keep it a priority. A ministerium must see this time of prayer as a non-negotiable step towards unity.

Programs will not create unity. Retreats will not create unity. Conferences, motivational speakers, and workshops will not create unity. It is confession before the Lord, both individually and corporately which led to Modesto's unity. It was seeking His face without an agenda or time line which served to enhance unity more than any other ingredient.

As II Chronicles 7:14 says,

"If my people, who are called by my name, will humble themselves and pray and seek my face and turn from their wicked ways, then will I hear from heaven and will forgive their sin and will heal their land."

Praying together served to unite the Greater Modesto Ministerial Association in many areas, however one of the greatest benefits of time together was that it solidified bonds of friendship. It created a sense that the pastors were on the "same team" rather than living in different kingdoms. Worshipping, singing, praying, sharing communion, and laughing together all enhanced a growing commitment to unity in the essentials while it strengthened an acceptance of diversity in the non-essentials.

Viewing pastors as members of one city wide pastoral staff is an awesome yet attainable goal for any community. The Wednesday prayer time offers a weekly "staff prayer time", a time to "huddle" which creates a team spirit.

Praying a blessing on people, Christian or not, represents the heart of God. Through the Lighthouses of Prayer crusade each Christian, pastors and lay people alike, were encouraged to pray blessings on the people within their "sphere of influence". They were learning to "talk to God about their neighbors before they talked to their neighbors about God".

SECTION THREE

Parachurch in a Supporting Role

CHAPTER 7.   CLEAN
(Citizens Leading Effective Action Now)

CHAPTER 8.   MODESTO UNION GOSPEL MISSION

CHAPTER 9.   PROMISE KEEPERS

In the area of parachurch organizations, CLEAN offers a platform for ministries which local churches often do not have either the resources or the motivation to operate. Ministries like CLEAN which target sexual addictions, political activities, or even hosting special political focused events offer the Christian community opportunities to pool their resources and accomplish goals which couldn't be accomplished individually. CLEAN also offers neutral territory for church members to gather and serve in a common and worthy cause.

The purpose of a city wide church is not to focus on political goals such as CLEAN has accomplished. The primary focus of the COM has always been to lift up the name of Jesus Christ. CLEAN represents the work of the Holy Spirit moving in the hearts of individuals within the COM to cooperate as members of one body, rather than separate congregations. They arrived at this point because their primary focus was to lift up the name of Christ rather than a political agenda. Their success in the political arena followed their success in the spiritual arena of prayer.

Another organization which provides giving and serving opportunities for Christians from different churches on is the Modesto Union Gospel Mission. Over 60 churches serve at

the Gospel Mission on a regular basis. This grass roots service opportunity develops a citywide unity at the most fundamental level. People involved in a Gospel Mission have
a jump start on unity by the mere nature of their ministry.

Other parachurch ministries, such as Promise Keepers,
need not be a threat to the local church or to the cause of
community church unity. In Modesto, the parachurch ministries have supported the local churches and been part of
the unity movement. If parachurch organizations are committed to local churches and their reason for existence is to
support the church then a mutual symbiotic relationship can
exist. Also, effective lay leadership in parachurch organizations often empowers men to be more effective lay leaders
in their own church.

Having the laypeople in a community be at the forefront
of such a unity movement is crucial. Christian men and
women who are leaders in their homes and churches must
also stand up and lead in the community.

SECTION FOUR

Partnering Together in Ministry

The initial cooperative follow-up effort of the Heavens Gates and Hell's Flames events were not planned by the church leaders. The cooperation was a reaction to the overwhelming response of the people to a moving of God's Spirit. When God wants to move us in a new direction or cause us to work together, He can make it happen. Not only was there cooperation, there was an absence of a competitive spirit in the Modesto churches. The Holy Spirit found fallow ground in Modesto to reap a great harvest through the Calvary Temple crusade.

God also found willing people to work in the harvest. The drama used untrained players from the local church, not a highly skilled traveling drama team. God desires and deserves all the credit for spiritual revival. In this instance it can truly be said that God used the foolish things of this world to confound the wise.

As of 1998, the Calvary Temple Drama had been witnessed by over 130,000 people during its 57 performances. God has used those performances to move 52,500 individuals to some form of decision for Christ.

Racial reconciliation has also been an integral part of Modesto's unity movement. One pastor stated that people should not be encouraged to attend churches along economical or racial lines. As a united church, Modesto is attempting to erase social, racial and economic lines. The COM's desire is that believers attend anywhere they feel God's leading and ultimately worship as one body of believers.

An event such as Meeting At The Tracks provided a useful and necessary tool in race reconciliation and community wide church unity. It broke down some racial walls as well as began building some relational bridges in Modesto. The important thing for any community with a heart for racial reconciliation is to begin somewhere, for Modesto that beginning was the "Meeting at the Tracks".

For a ministerium to succeed at racial reconciliation, it's leadership must be of an ethnic mix and meetings should not always be on "white turf." Larger churches must be willing to share the leadership of the ministerial association with smaller church pastors. It must be shared among ethnic churches as well.

The stadium event gave the people of Modesto an opportunity to operate as "one church", and for a significant cause as well. Though a small amount of money in terms of the larger national picture, this project was significant for the local churches, both black and white.

The stadium event provided an opportunity for the COM to do something tangible toward racial reconciliation. The $33,000 offering at the 1996 event toward the burned churches relief fund demonstrated the Church of Modesto's heart for racial reconciliation.

As communities, churches need to develop cooperative policies and stand together with them. Some examples of these are the Community Marriage Policy and church discipline issues.

The community marriage policy was one of the first building blocks of unity within the ministerium. It provided a common concern that all pastors could agree on. Second to prayer, a community marriage policy is a good starting point in working toward unity. As Mike McManus stated, "Churches can cooperate across denominational lines to save marriages."

A community marriage policy has impacted the divorce rate in Modesto. It can do the same in any community willing to cooperate in a similar way. Mike McManus and Jim Talley are two nationally know leaders who are willing to assist any community in developing a community marriage policy.

Though a more recent aspect of Modesto's story, the Youth Pastors Network is an active and signifigant part of the unity movement. It is essential for the youth workers in a community to cooperate for the sake of the next generation. They must break down walls formed by competitive spirits in order for the next generation to experience the blessings of unity. As Rick Fritzmeyer of Youth For Christ stated, "Absence of conflict is not the goal, learning to love each other is".

SECTION FIVE

Projects Together in Service

CHAPTER 15   THE FLOODS OF 97 AND "GMAC"

CHAPTER 16   "CHURCH BURNING RELIEF"

Natural disasters provide excellent opportunities for a community's churches to rally together and demonstrate Christ's compassion and unity within the Body of Christ. It is essential by the very nature of disasters that the churches respond quickly to the crisis.

In the case of the Modesto Flood of '97, it was a wise decision of the GMMA to hire an outside administrator, Tom Van Groningen, to run the operation. Had any one church directed the work, it would have limited the efforts for obvious reasons.

Involving community organizations and government agencies was a wise and effective decision on the part of GMAC. Without the resources provided by these agencies, the total relief project may never have been successfully completed. It also enabled the church to be "salt and light" to a spectrum of our society which normally has very little interaction with the Christian church.

Though a small amount of money in terms of the larger national picture, this project was significant for the local churches, both black and white. It provided an opportunity for the COM to do something tangible toward racial reconciliation.

It is important to start somewhere in the process of race reconciliation. The key is to start, God will direct the process once a community steps foreward in obedience.

SECTION SIX

Conclusion

Church unity, like racial unity, is a process that takes years of hard work and prayer. In Modesto it has been in process for several decades. The first noted effort occurred in 1948 with the Billy Graham Crusade.

Any movement which involves a large number of people will experience detractors. Usually there is a thread of truth is any criticism, therefore it is prudent to carefully consider the criticism and find any truth in it, then make the appropriate adjustments. Modesto's movement has experienced criticism from several directions, yet the pastors have remained committed to God's call toward spiritual unity within His local Modesto body.

For city wide unity to occur, pastors must possess a sense of calling to a city, not simply to a church. A result of this commitment seen in the long serving tenures by many of Modesto's ministers.

Accomplishing projects has not been the primary purpose of unity, bringing glory to God has!

God is not willing to share his glory with any one. Modesto's pastors have been modest about the recognition Modesto has received, and have recognized that God is the one responsible for all which has occurred in their community.

The potential Modesto possessed for city wide church unity is available for any community. God's desires do not change and his heart still beats for unity within his church. While the flood was a natural disaster and the Calvary Temple play was a supernatural moving of the Holy Spirit, most of Modesto's experiences have been a result of God blessing the faithfulness in prayer and hard work together in ministry. This is evidence that with willing hearts and faithful consistent leadership, community wide church unity is possible in any community.

CONCLUSION

After numerous interviews, much research, combined with the personal experience of sharing in each of these chapters, the author believes it is both valuable and important to answer two questions.

1. Is Modesto's experience transferable to another community?

2. Is it possible to reduce these concepts to three practical principles?

My reply is "Yes", and "Yes". I believe unity is God's desire for every community's churches. Unfortunately, unity is blocked by sin — either subtle sins of omission or blatant sins of comission. But when God's Spirit is pursued and unleashed in a community, unity will prevail.

I believe there are three principles which are transferable and would carry a community a great distance down unity's path. Those three are:

1. Prayer in many venues, but especially corporately by the pastors and leaders.
2. Partnership. Working together on local community needs as God leads.
3. Persistence over many years.

Modesto's process has been grounded in five years of weekly prayer meetings by its pastors, in fifteen years of consistent leadership within the Ministerial Association, and a fifty year history of slowly working in the direction of unity.

Yes, unity is possible for the churches in your community!

Chapter 18

SCRIPTURAL STUDY ON CHURCH UNITY

As ONE INVESTIGATES more carefully what scripture says on the subject of church unity it becomes clear that this is a very important issue to our Heavenly Father. It is especially important in light of the relationship within the Godhead, the perfect model of unity. Five key aspects of church unity to be considered are:

I.   CHRISTIAN UNITY IS BLOCKED BY A SPIRIT OF INDEPENDENCE!   Haggai 1:1-11

II.   CHRISTIAN UNITY BEARS A RESEMBLANCE TO THE GODHEAD!   John 17 & Ephesians 4:1-6

III.   CHRISTIAN UNITY IS BASED ON WHAT CHRIST HAS DONE!   Selected Passages

IV. CHRISTIAN UNITY BELONGS TO EACH BELIEVER!
                                                    John 17:20-26

V.   CHRISTIAN UNITY BENEFITS EVERYONE!
                                                    Psalm 133:1-3

I. CHRISTIAN UNITY IS BLOCKED BY
A SPIRIT OF INDEPENDENCE!

Haggai 1:1-11

1. In the second year of King Darius, on the first day of the sixth month, the word of the LORD came through the prophet Haggai to Zerubbabel son of Shealtiel, governor of Judah, and to Joshua son of Jehozadak, the high priest.

2. This is what the LORD Almighty says:

> *"These people say, 'The time has not yet come*
> > *for the LORD's house to be built.' "*

3. Then the word of the LORD came
> > through the prophet Haggai:

4. *"Is it a time for you yourselves*
> *to be living in your paneled houses,*
> > *while this house remains a ruin?"*

5. Now this is what the LORD Almighty says:

> *"Give careful thought to your ways."*

6.   *You have planted much, but have harvested little.*
> *You eat, but never have enough.*
> > *You drink, but never have your fill.*
> > *You put on clothes, but are not warm.*
> > > *You earn wages,*
> > > > *only to put them in a purse with holes in it."*

7. This is what the LORD Almighty says:
> > *"Give careful thought to your ways.*

8. *Go up into the mountains and bring down timber and build the house, so that I may take pleasure in it and be honored,"* says the LORD.

9. *"You expected much, but see, it turned out to be little. What you brought home, I blew away. Why?"* declares the LORD Almighty. *"Because of My house, which remains a ruin, while each of you is busy with his own house.*

10. *Therefore, because of you the heavens have withheld their dew and the earth its crops.*

11. *I called for a drought on the fields and the mountains, on the grain, the new wine, the oil and whatever the ground produces, on men and cattle, and on the labor of your hands."*

A. The criticism from God.

1. *"Is it a time for you yourselves to be living in your paneled houses, while this house remains a ruin?"*
(v.4)

Speaking through the Prophet Haggai to the Israelites, God was saying that they were focusing too much attention on their own houses to the neglect of the house of God. One present day application could be that our pastors and church leaders are focusing too much attention on their own church facility and program, and neglecting the greater church of God in their communities. We get tunnel vision and lose sight of the needs of the churches down the street. Being part of God's family is larger than the membership of our own particular congregation.

2. *"You have planted much, but have harvested little."*
(v.6)

In today's setting, our churches have invested much energy in evangelism and church growth with little to show for our efforts. Millions are spent on crusades, outreaches, concerts, and buildings in America. Still church growth experts tell us we are not keeping up with population growth statistics. In fact, " American church attendance in a given week during 1996 was down to 37 percent of the population, a ten year low . . . even though 82 percent of Americans claim to be Christians".[40] And this trend continues today. It is a valid indictment, yes, as churches we are planting much and harvesting little.

B. The cause of spiritual drought.

> *"What you brought home, I blew away. Why?"* declares the LORD Almighty. *"Because of My house, which remains a ruin, while each of you is busy with his own house."* (v.9)

Most churches are so busy with their own programs and buildings that they have little time or energy left to invest in the bigger picture of God's world wide church. Our nearsightedness actually weakens our own churches as well as the greater kingdom of God.

C. The cure of the spiritual drought.

> *"Go up into the mountains and bring down timber and build the house, so that I may take pleasure in it and be honored,"* says the LORD. (v. 8)

Haggai clarifies what will end this drought. It was to rebuild God's house, God's temple in Jerusalem. In todays setting, God wants the local churches to begin focusing more attention on the bigger picture of unity, on breaking down walls and building bridges. He has a desire to see His church saturate the world with the Gospel, which begins when churches have a vision to saturate their city with the Gospel. Yes, each church must focus more energy beyond it's own boundaries. That energy must focus on both local efforts as well as world wide mission if the world is to be reached. Certainly God will take greater pleasure when His church places a higher priority on a united effort at building His kingdom.

Remember God's exhortation through the Prophet Haggai: *". . . bring down timber and build the house, so that I may take pleasure in it and be honored"*.

II. CHRISTIAN UNITY BEARS A RESEMBLANCE TO THE GODHEAD!

John 17 & Ephesians 4:1-6

John 17 provides a perfect model for our unity. It is a passage which portrays the relationship within the Godhead as a one of singlemindedness. It could also be described as a relationship of oneness in purpose or unity.

A. Unity's pattern is seen in the Godhead.

> The unity of the church expressed in our Lord's prayer in John 17, is not the kind of unity that is being touted by the World Council of Churches. They have tried to reduce the elements of faith to the lowest common denominator. True unity is not sought by pretending there are no differences, as modern ecumenists have done, but by recognizing and respecting those differences, while focusing on the great orthodox truths all Christians share.[41]

The pattern seen in the Godhead is a pattern of unity in purpose as seen in the work they share in verse four. *"I have brought you glory on earth by completing the work you gave me to do."* In verse five one sees the glory they have shared from eternity past: *"And now, Father, glorify me in your presence with the glory I had with you before the world began."*

Their unity of possessions is seen in verse ten. *"All I have is yours, and all you have is mine. And glory has come to me through them."* What a perfect model of unity for the church! If the church could only be unified in it's work, it's glory, and it's possessions, instead of duplicating so much effort and so many resources. What a shame and what a waste!

B. Unity's purpose is to prepare the world for evangelism.

In John 17:21, God shows His intended purpose for unity. John writes: *"That the world may believe...."* Glen Wagner observes that community-wide church unity does have an impact on evangelism. It results in greater effectiveness in ministry.

> Could it be that the church in the United States is barely keeping up with the population because of a lack of unity? Could our lack of unity be contributing to the moral decline we are experiencing...? We are not transforming the culture. The culture is transforming us. It is time to reverse that trend. That is unity's purpose.[42]

In Modesto the Lighthouses of Prayer were designed to pave the way for Christians to share the Gospel of Christ with their nearby neighbors and friends. The unity of churches working together in this citywide outreach was for the primary purpose of evangelism.

C. Unity's power is unleashed through the Church to do evangelism.

"You will receive power when the Holy Spirit comes on you, and you will be My witnesses in Jerusalem, and in all Judea and Samaria, and to all the ends of the earth."   Acts 1:8

This is a spiritual power which infects the world. As Glen Wagner describes it:

> "The mobilization of an army with a common pattern and purpose, and an awesome power."[43]

In Modesto's case, unity did serve to unleash God's power in the direction of evangelism. There have been many miraculous stories of people meeting Christ through interdenominational teamwork. The citywide evangelism effort, combined with the radio and television broadcast, introduced many people to Christ. God's power has been especially evident throughout the ministry of Calvary Temple's play, *Heaven's Gates and Hell's Flames*, with many stories documented earlier in this study. Pastor Glenn Berteau reports that a total of one hundred thirty thousand people have witnessed the play, with fifty two thousand five hundred individuals professing some sort of decision for Christ.

D. Unity's practice is that we walk in a manner worthy of our calling.

Eph. 4:1-6

> 1. *"As a prisoner for the Lord, then, I urge you to live a life worthy of the calling you have received.*
> 2. *Be completely humble and gentle; be patient, bearing with one another in love.*
> 3. *Make every effort to keep the unity of the Spirit through the bond of peace.*
> 4. *There is one body and one Spirit– just as you were called to one hope when you were called –*
> 5. *one Lord, one faith, one baptism;*
> 6. *one God and Father of all, who is over all and through all and in all."*

1. Unity's character qualities are humility, gentleness, patience, and tolerance.

Do these characterize the relationships within the body of Christ? Does the Christian church posess a reputation of gentleness and patience toward one another? What if they truly did?

2. Unity's challenge is to maintain a bond of peace as we see in verse three.

Why has the church been depicted so often as an organization with manifold divisions. The distinctives of our particular denominations have been of higher importance than our distinctives as children of God, which are the very things which unite us. Yes, it remains a challenge to maintain a bond of peace within the church when we are so divided over interpretive issues.

3. Unity's calling is to one hope.

Our hope is the same regardless of whether we attend a Baptist or Brethren, an Evangelical Free or Episcopal, or even a Presbyterian or Pentecostal. Our Lord is the same Lord and our hope the same hope. Since that hope unites us, let us draw together in the other areas Christ has given us to share. As one man observed, there are no strangers in foxholes, and the church must recognize who the enemy truly is. It is time to rally together before it is too late.

III.   CHRISTIAN UNITY IS BASED ON WHAT CHRIST HAS DONE!
Selected Passages

The following eight aspects to the unity of the church are spiritual blessings members of God's family all share in common resulting from Christ's finished work on the cross. As Christians we are truly a blessed and wealthy people.

A. He placed us in one body.

As the world-wide Church of Jesus Christ we are part of the same body. Our first allegiance should always be to His body, that larger world-wide Church. When the Modesto Ministerium refers to "His Church," that is what it is referring to. The Greater Modesto Ministerium Association states its purpose is: "To exalt the Lord Jesus Christ by working together to build His church and obey His Word, while recognizing our distinctives in the body of Christ."   Modesto Ministerium Purpose Statement

B. He filled us with the same spirit.

"Set his seal of ownership on us, and put his Spirit in our hearts as a deposit, guaranteeing what is to come."   II Corinthians 1:22

"There are different kinds of gifts, but the same Spirit."   First Corinthians 12:4

The scripture is clear in presenting the point that the church is indwelt by the same spirit, the Spirit of God. Since this is true, we the church are so intimately related it leaves no room for behavior which is less than loving family interaction. God leaves us no choices other than loving, supporting and interacting with other churches who serve the same Jesus as we do.

What a joy for the 9,000 Christians who attended the Modesto stadium events to sense the unity in God's Spirit as they worshipped together. People left those evenings inspired by Holy Spirit's presence in a manner few Christians have been privileged to experience.

C. He has provided us with one hope.

"Praise be to the God and Father of our Lord Jesus Christ! In His great mercy He has given us new birth into a living hope through the resurrection of Jesus Christ from the dead.   I Peter 1:3

Few things unite people as much as a common hope. Whether its a hope that a severe drought will end, to that a sports team will come out on top, or more importantly, a loved one will regain their health. That shared hope draws people together when few other things will. That is just the case with the church. Our shared hope of life after death and in the return of the Lord Jesus Christ should unite Christians from different churches like nothing else.

D. He has given us the same destiny.

> *"We are called to be conformed to the image of His Son which will occur when we see the glorified Christ."*   Romans 8:29

Our destiny of a glorified body and a heavenly home provides a common future we as believers all share. No matter what different challenges and directions life holds for us individually, all who name the name of Christ as Savior are destined to spend eternity together in the presence of the Savior inhabiting glorified bodies. Since Christians are going to spend eternity together in heaven, that hope should motivate Christians and churches to prepare for that time by loving one another now.

E. He is our Lord, we worship the same Master

> *"There is salvation in no one else for there is no other name that has been given among men by which we must be saved."*   Acts 4:12

Christians of all denominations and churches worship the same Lord. The beauty of Christ is that He is big enough to allow for many varieties of worship styles. He inhabits the praises of His people, the sincere praises of His people.

F. His word and work have provided us with one faith.

"The faith which was once for all delivered to the saints and for which we contend."   Jude 3

We take our instruction from the same source. We must accept the Bible as God's Word. Accepting the Scripture as God-breathed is one of the absolutes which churches must agree upon to experience genuine Christian fellowship.

G. His death, burial, and resurrection is the basis for one baptism.

"One Lord, one faith, one baptism." Ephesians 4:5

The early church believers were not baptized in the name of their local church or in an apostle, but in the name of Christ. Scripture places much emphasis upon water baptism.

H. He is our only God and Father.

We are children of the same Father, as seen in First Corinthians 8:4-6

> 4. *So then, about eating food sacrificed to idols: We know that an idol is nothing at all in the world and that there is no God but one.*
> 5. *For even if there are so-called gods, whether in heaven or on earth (as indeed there are many "gods" and many "lords"),*
> 6. *yet for us there is but one God, the Father, from whom all things came and for whom we live; and there is but one Lord, Jesus Christ, through whom all things came and through whom we live.*

[Outline Borrowed from: Seifert, David, Tape Series: Ephesians – Reaching our Highest Potential #8 *"How to keep your relationships together"*]

IV. CHRISTIAN UNITY BELONGS TO
EACH BELIEVER!
JOHN 17:20-26

In John 17 we see a wonderful example and outline of
unity in Jesus' prayer to the Father.

A. We trust in the same Savior.

*I pray also for those who will believe in Me through
the Word.*   John 17:20

B. We bare the same witness to the world.

*"That they may all be one just as You are in Me
and I in You. May they also be in Us so that the
world may believe that You sent Me."*   John 17:22

Twice in this prayer our Savior refers to the church's
witness to the lost. Our witness is constantly under scrutiny from the world. The unchurched are
watching Christians' lives and looking for reality.
One thing which convinces them there isn't any
is the bickering and division within Christian
churches they see. Yet by the same token, one
of the most powerful testimonies of Christianity's
reality to the outside world is our unity!

It doesn't matter what church you attend. When
you are on the front lines sharing your faith with
someone, the plan of salvation stays the same. We
share the same witness of a loving God who came
to save needy mankind.

C. We possess the same glory

*"And the glory which You gave Me I have given
them."*   John 17:22, 24

What an honor to share our Heavenly Father's
glory with Him and with one another. This is truly
a mystery!

D. We enjoy the same love.

"That the world may know that You have loved them as You have loved Me." John 17:23

Each person is greatly loved. God's love for mankind is limitless. One privilege God has shared with me is the opportunity to travel and visit Christians in several parts of the world. Seeing the love of God in the faces of Christians in dark Godless cultures is a remarkable and unmistakable sight. His love is truly life changing to experience.

V. CHRISTIAN UNITY BENEFITS EVERYONE!

Psalm 133:1-3

> 1. *How good and pleasant it is when brothers live together in unity!*
> 2. *It is like precious oil poured on the head, running down on the beard, running down on Aaron's beard, down upon the collar of his robes.*
> 3. *It is as if the dew of Hermon were falling on Mount Zion. For there the LORD bestows his blessing, even life forevermore.*

Dr. David Seifert's numerous Holy Land tours have provided him with an interesting perspective on the unity described in Psalm 133. In an earlier interview recorded for this study, he illustrates Psalm 133 this way:

I think one of the critical passages that needs to be developed is Psalm 133:1 *"Behold, how good and how pleasant, how sweet it is when brothers dwell together in unity."* And that Psalm goes on to say that it like the dew coming off of Mt. Hermon. When you've been to Israel, there's a number of things that strike you. One is Mt. Hermon. It is nearly 10,000 feet high, and seated right there above where the Jordan River starts.

If you stop and think about it, the clouds of precipitation and the fog come in from the Mediterranean, they hit that high mountain and condense into precipitation. It rains, the water runs down to where the head waters of the Jordan River begin. That one mountain gives life to the entire nation. It's fascinating when you begin to understand that fact. God says its like the dew off of Mt. Hermon when brothers and sisters dwell together in unity, that there is a blessing just like Mt. Hermon is for the entire nation of Israel. God says, *"There I will command my blessing."*

Unity is a wonderful thing to experience but a difficult thing to maintain. The apostle Paul exhorts the church to *"be diligent to preserve the unity of the Spirit in the bond of peace"* (Eph. 4:3). He says that because unity takes work! There is no easy path leading there. We must move fast and work hard to create unity and to maintain what we have in Christ.

Certainly there are many great blessings which are derived from unity, but here are three of the most important ones:

A. Unity releases power to accomplish God's will on this earth.

Unity releases power to live the way God has called us to live. It releases power which is untapped apart from this avenue of unity. The flood relief effort in Modesto is an excellent example of unity's power to accomplish mighty tasks in the name of Christ. Hundreds of homes were reconstructed in a spirit of harmony. Work, which could not have been accomplished apart from the unity God has blessed the Church of Modesto with enabling them to work together. This great work was done when God's power was released in His name.

B. Unity attracts the blessings of God.

Clearly the preeminent blessing of Psalm 133 is "life forever." But there are blessings which only come from this type of fellowship, ones which are intangible and only experienced by those who have traveled this path. The blessings of joy and intimacy and support from people who were formerly distant and skeptical. What a blessing to move beyond those barriers.

For over five years Modesto's pastors have been growing closer and closer together in the bond of love and unity. This growth has come during their annual prayer summits and weekly prayer meetings. These are men who prior to the prayer summits were at best professionally courteous to one another. Miraculously, today they are genuinely good friends and prayer partners. For them the blessings of joy and intimacy are no longer a distant dream but a living reality. King David's description of the glory of unity in Psalm 133 is truly descriptive of the pastor's Prayer Summits.

C. Unity captures the attention of an unbelieving world.

There is no doubt that the community of Modesto, California, has recognized that the churches of their community have come together in a new way in the past five years. This study, with special focus on the Mayor's interview, demonstrates that God has used the unity of the Church of Modesto to attract the community's attention. As Modesto's Mayor Lang stated, other communities mayors are aware of the cooperation between Modesto and it's churches and wish they had the same relationship.

Over the past five years several national news programs have also featured different aspects of the Church of Modesto. Many stories have focused specifically on the Community Marriage Policy while others mentioned the Calvary Temple play. Attracting the world's attention was God's purpose for the ancient Nation of Israel. Their "family spirit" was to communicate and attract those around them into fellowship with their compassionate Deity. God's heart for the world remains the same today. The church is to reflect that same "family spirit" so all who care to look will be attracted to our compassionate "Deity," our heavenly Father and His Son, Jesus Christ. Unity's greatest purpose is to attract the world's attention to focus on a loving God and His message of redemption.

The Church of Modesto

NOTES

1. **Max Lucado,** *In the Grip of Grace,*
(Word Publishing, 1996,) pp. 160-163.

2. **"300 Most Favorable Cities in America,"** *Modesto Bee,*
20 August, 1995, Section A-1, p. 1.

3. **Dick Lang,** "Church of Modesto," Interview #01
at Mayor's office, Modesto, CA, recorded Aug. 20, 1998.

4. **C.S. Lewis,** *Letters: C.S. Lewis/ Don Giovanni Calabria,*
Translated and edited by Martin Moynihan (Ann Arbor, Mich.:
Servant Books,1988.) para. 3, pp. 37, 39 (25 Nov. 1947).

5. **Billy Graham,** *Just As I Am,*
San Francisco, Harper - Collins Pub., 1997.

6. **Cliff Barrows,** "Church of Modesto," Interview #02
by phone from North Carolina, recorded Sept. 3, 1998.

7. **Peter Johansen,** "Church of Modesto," Interview #03
at Peter Johansen's home, Modesto, recorded June 12, 1998.

8. **Dr. David Seifert,** "Church of Modesto," Interview #04
at Dr. Seifert's office, Modesto, CA, recorded Aug. 11, 1998.

9. **C.S. Lewis,** *Letters: ... ibid.*
para. 5, pp. 37, 39 (25 Nov. 1947.)

10. **Ross Briles,** "Church of Modesto," Interview #05
at Jim Bouck's office, Modesto, CA, recorded June 10, 1998.

11. **Wade Estes,** "Church of Modesto," Interview #06
at Wade Estes' office, Modesto, CA, recorded Aug. 18, 1998.

12. **Ed Silvoso,** "Church of Modesto," Interview #07
by phone from San Francisco, CA, recorded Aug. 13, 1998.

13. Todd Hunnicutt, "Church of Modesto," Interview questions were responded to in written form, Modesto, Aug. 10, 1998. q.v. Appendices A & B.

14. Ed Silvoso, *That None Should Perish,*
(Ventura, CA: Regal Books, 1994), p. 57.

15. Ed Silvoso *ibid,* p. 21.

16. C.S. Lewis, *Mere Christianity,*
(New York, Macmillan, 1952.) bk. III, chap. 3, par. 4, p. 80.

17. Harry Kullijian, "Church of Modesto," Interview #08 at Harry Kullijian's home, Modesto, CA, recorded Aug. 5, 1998.

18. Barbara Deatherage, "Church of Modesto," Interview #09 at Modesto, California, recorded August 10, 1998.

19. Steven Kremer, "Church of Modesto," Interview #10 at Jim Bouck's office, Modesto, CA, recorded Aug. 21, 1998.

20. C.S. Lewis, *God in the Dock; Essays on Theology and Ethics.* Edited by Walter Hooper. (Grand Rapids, Michigan.: Eerdmans, 1970.) "Answers to Questions on Christianity" (1944), ans. 14, p. 60.

21. Susan Childress, "Prayer Yelds Bountiful Harvest".
Christianity Today, June 19, 1995.

22. Glen Berteau, "Church of Modesto," Interview #11 at Glen Berteau's office, Modesto, CA, recorded Aug. 21, 1998.

23. Susan Childress, "Testimoniess From The Drama Heaven's Gates & Hell's Flames". *Calvary Temple Newsletter,* April, 1995.

24. Glen Berteau, *When God Shakes a City.*
Springfield, Missouri: Gospel Publishing House, 1997) p. 163.

25. Darius Crosby, "Church of Modesto," Interview #12 at Jim Bouck's home, Modesto, CA, recorded Aug. 21, 1998.

26. Charlie Crane, "Church of Modesto," Interview #13 at Jim Bouck's office, Modesto, CA, recorded Feb. 10, 1998.

27. Cliff Traub, "Church of Modesto," Interview #14 at Cliff Traub's office, Modesto, CA, recorded Aug. 17, 1998.

28. Michael J. McManus, *Marriage Savers*, (Grand Rapids: Zondervan Publishing, 1993, '95), pp. 302-303.

29. Michael McManus, *Marriage Savers Newsletter*, (Bethesda, Maryland: Summer, 1998.)

30. Jim Talley, "Church of Modesto," Interview #15 by phone from Oklahoma City, Oklahoma, recorded Aug. 14, 1998.

31. Michael McManus, "Church of Modesto," Interview #16 by phone from Bethesda, Maryland, recorded Aug. 12, 1998.

32. US Health Statistics, Washington DC, 1998.

33. Stanislaus County Recorders Office, March, 1999.

34. Rick Fritzmeyer, "Church of Modesto," Interview #17 at the Youth for Christ office, recorded Aug. 18, 1998.

35. Peter Scholtes, Words and Music Copyright ©1966 by F.E.L. Publications

36. Tom Van Groningen and Bill Reit, "Church of Modesto," Interview #18 at GMAC offices, Modesto, CA, recorded Feb. 23, 1998.

37. Jeff Kreiser, "Church of Modesto," Interview #19 at Jeff Kreiser's office, Modesto, CA, recorded Aug. 17, 1998.

38. John Winthrop, *Model of Christian Charity*, 1630 (Boston: Massachusetts Historical Society, 1931) Vol. II, pp. 292-295.

39. C.S. Lewis, *Mere Christianity*, (New York, Macmillan, 1952.)

40. Jim Cymbala, *Fresh Wind, Fresh Fire*, (Grand Rapids: Zondervan Publishing House, 1997.) pg. 90.

41. Chuck Colson, *The Body,* (Dallas: Word Publishing, 1997) p. 104.

42. Glenn Wagner, *The Awesome Power Of Shared Beliefs,* (Dallas: Word Publishing, 1997) p. 27.

43. Ibid., p.27.

The Church of Modesto

BIBLIOGRAPHY

Books

Berteau, Glen. *When God Shakes A City.*
(Springfield, Missouri: Gospel Publishing House, 1997.)

Colson, Chuck. *The Body.* (Dallas: Word Publishing, 1997.)

Cymbala, Jim. *Fresh Wind, Fresh Fire.*
(Grand Rapids: Zondervan Publishing House, 1997.)

Graham, Billy. *Just As I Am.*
(San Francisco: Harper-Collins Pub., 1997.)

Lewis, C.S. *God in the Dock; Essays on Theology and Ethics.*
Edited by Walter Hooper. (Grand Rapids, Michigan: Eerdmans, 1970.)

Lewis, C.S. *Letters: C.S. Lewis / Don Giovanni Calabria.*
Translated and edited by Martin Moynihan. (Ann Arbor, Michigan: Servant Books, 1988.)

Lewis, C.S. *Mere Christianity.* (New York: Macmillan, 1952.)

Lucado, Max. *In the Grip of Grace.* (Word Publishing, 1996,)

McManus, Michael J. *Marriage Savers.*
(Grand Rapids: Zondervan Publishing, 1993, 1995.)

Silvoso, Ed. *That None Should Perish.*
(Ventura, California: Regal Books, 1994.)

Books (continued)

Wagner, Glenn. *The Awesome Power Of Shared Beliefs.*
(Dallas: Word Publishing, 1997.)

Winthrop, John. *Model of Christian Charity.* 1630
(Boston: Massachusetts Historical Society, 1931.)

Periodicals

Childress, Susan. "Prayer Yields Bountiful Harvest."
Christianity Today, June 19, 1995.

Childress, Susan. "Testimonies From The Drama Heaven's Gates
& Hell's Flames." *Calvary Temple Newsletter,* April, 1995.

McManus, Michael. *Marriage Savers Newsletter.*
(Bethesda, Maryland: Summer, 1998.)

"300 Most Favorable Cities in America." *Modesto Bee,*
20 August, 1995, Section A-1.

The Church of Modesto

BIBLIOGRAPHY

Taped Interviews

Barrows, Cliff. "Church of Modesto," Interview #02 by phone from North Carolina, recorded September 3, 1998.

Berteau, Glen. "Church of Modesto," Interview #11 at Glen Berteau's office, Modesto, California, recorded August 21, 1998.

Briles, Ross. "Church of Modesto," Interview #05 at Jim Bouck's office, Modesto, California, recorded June 10, 1998.

Crane, Charlie. "Church of Modesto," Interview #13 at Jim Bouck's office, Modesto, California, recorded February 10, 1998.

Crosby, Darius. "Church of Modesto," Interview #12 at Jim Bouck's home, Modesto, California, recorded August 21, 1998.

Deatherage, Barbara. "Church of Modesto," Interview #09 at Modesto Gospel Mission, Modesto, California, recorded August 10, 1998.

Estes, Wade. "Church of Modesto," Interview #06 at Wade Estes' office, Modesto, California, recorded August 18, 1998.

Fritzmeyer, Rick. "Church of Modesto," Interview #17 the Youth for Christ office, Modesto, California, recorded August 18, 1998.

Hunnicutt, Todd. "Church of Modesto," Interview questions were responded to in written form on Aug. 10, 1998. Original document on file.

Johansen, Peter. "Church of Modesto," Interview #03 at Peter Johansen's home, Modesto, California, recorded June 12, 1998.

Kremer, Steven. "Church of Modesto," Interview #10 at Jim Bouck's office, Modesto, California, recorded February 19, 1998.

Kreiser, Jeff. "Church of Modesto," Interview #19 at Jim Bouck's office, Modesto, California, recorded August 17, 1998.

Kullijan, Harry. "Church of Modesto," Interview #08 at Harry Kullijan's home, Modesto, California, recorded August 5, 1998.

Lang, Dick. "Church of Modesto," Interview #01 at Mayors office, Modesto, California, recorded August 20, 1998.

McManus, Michael. "Church of Modesto," Interview #16 by phone from Bethesda, Maryland, recorded August 12, 1998.

Seifert, Dr. David. "Church of Modesto," Interview #04 at Dr. Seifert's office, Modesto, California, recorded August 11, 1998.

Silvoso, Ed. "Church of Modesto," Interview #07 by phone from San Francisco, California, recorded August 13, 1998.

Talley, Jim. "Church of Modesto," Interview #15 by phone from Oklahoma City, Oklahoma, recorded August 14, 1998.

Traub, Cliff. "Church of Modesto," Interview #14 at Cliff Traub's office, Modesto, California, recorded August 17, 1998.

Van Groningen, Tom. "Church of Modesto," Interview #18 at the GMAC offices, Modesto, California, recorded February 23, 1998.

The Church of Modesto

APPENDIX A

Interview Questions

1. Introduce yourself, please, and give a little of your background and how you are related to the Church of Modesto. Give a thumbnail sketch of your area of ministry.

2. How did your ministry contribute to the great sense of unity the Church of Modesto is experiencing today?

3. Who were the key people who played a part in your ministry? What roles did they play?

4. Had God done anything in your heart to prepare you personally for this movement of unity?

5. Were there any bench mark events or statistics in your area of ministry what contributed to the Church of Modesto?

6. Would you share any supernatural experiences in which God demonstrated His handiwork in causing this movement?

7. Why do you think God chose to begin such a work in our city?

8. Do you see any down sides to the Church of Modesto movement?

9. What lessons or principles have you observed here in Modesto which could help other communities bring their churches together?

The Church of Modesto

APPENDIX B

Contact Information

Church of Modesto Website: www.churchofmodesto.org

Bob Cryder   503/238-4728

e-mail   www.bobcryder@compuserve.com

Michael J. McManus   Marriage Savers
                            9500 Michael's Ct.
                            Bethesda, MD   20817

301/469-5873   FAX 301/469-5871

Dr. Jim Talley   405/720-8300

Website: www.drtalley.com

e-mail   drtalley@drtalley.com